THE
POWER
OF
ZU

A MARDUKITE SYSTEMOLOGY PUBLICATION

Mardukite Research Library Catalogue No. "Liber S1-Z"
Systemology Air Command Reports #21DEC19–#06JAN20

Published from
Mardukite Borsippa HQ, San Luis Valley, Colorado
Founding Church of Mardukite Zuism,
Mardukite Academy & Systemology Society

Cover Graphics and Systemology Logos by Kyra Kaos

MARDUKITE ACADEMY OF SYSTEMOLOGY PREMIERE EDITION

THE POWER OF

ZU

APPLYING MARDUKITE ZUISM AND SYSTEMOLOGY TO EVERYDAY LIFE

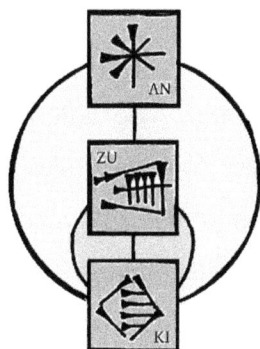

Based on the original lectures
by Joshua Free
as introduced by Reed Penn

JOSHUA FREE
publishing imprint

© 2021, JOSHUA FREE

ISBN : 978-0-578-92445-8

SYSTEMOLOGY

*Transcripts for the Lecture Series
given to the Systemology Society in
December 2019, originally titled:
Keys to Increasing Control of
the Radiant Energy in Everyday Life*

Premiere Hardcover Collector's Edition—July 2021

mardukite.com

A Practical Approach to Spiritual Technology

We exist at the threshold of a true New Age, standing to witness first rays of a Crystal Dawn on the horizon. Sparks of clear light from the forthcoming Crystal Age peek out to awaken the first seeds and cells of Earth to a new realization. It signals an inception of the Coming Race—a new era for a new type of metahuman.

Now a decade in the making behind-the-scenes—since *Systemology: The Original Thesis* quietly debuted in 2011 —Joshua Free emerges from the underground with a new public inception for *Mardukite Zuism & Systemology* and a new Mardukite Esoteric Research Library of concise, practical and effective spiritual technologies; new classics such as *Tablets of Destiny* and *Crystal Clear.*

Power of Zu documents the first introduction course given by Joshua Free to the Systemology Society. Candidly presenting the entire subject from scratch in a way anyone can understand, now you too can approach *Mardukite Zuism* and discover the underlying Systemology of all Existence exactly as experienced by advanced students and newcomers actually attending the three-day lecture series during December 2019.

This collector's edition hardcover publication includes complete transcripts to *all nine lectures*; an extended introduction by Reed Penn, describing discovery of *Spiritual Life Energy* in *Mardukite Zuism* and *Systemology* and concept of "ZU" in Sumerian cuneiform language; the "*Mardukite Zuism: A Brief Introduction*" discourse; and a newly revised glossary for easily referencing the specific meaning intended for nearly 200 terms used in these lecture transcripts, introducing concise practical fundamentals of *Mardukite Zuism* and *Systemology* as applied to everyday life in this Universe and beyond.

Welcome to 21st Century Mardukite New Thought

JOSHUA FREE'S
"THE POWER OF ZU" LECTURE SERIES
DECEMBER 2019

∞

EDITOR'S NOTE

"The Self does not actualize Awareness
past a point not understood."
—*Tablets of Destiny*

This book contains transcripts from an introductory
lecture series given by Joshua Free to new students
of the Systemology Society and Mardukite Alumni
in December 2019 at the release of "*Crystal Clear.*"

Wherever a word that is defined in the glossary
first appears in the transcripts, it will be **bold**.

A clear understanding of this material is critical for
achieving actual realizations and personal benefit
from applying philosophies of *Mardukite Zuism* and
NexGen Systemology spiritual technology.

The *Seeker* should be especially certain not to simply
"read through" this book without attaining proper
comprehension as "knowledge." Even when the
information continues to be "interesting"—if at any
point you find yourself feeling lost or confused while
reading, trace your steps back. Return to the point of
misunderstanding and go through it again.

Take nothing within this book on faith.
Apply the information directly to your life.

Decide for yourself.

∞

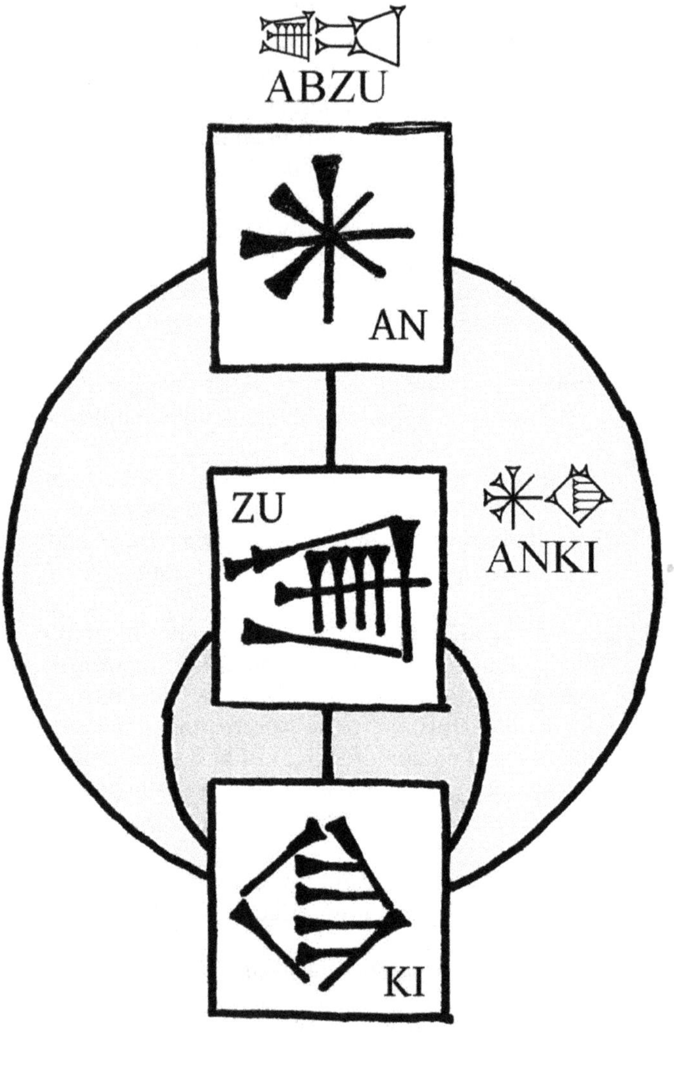
ABZU
AN
ZU
ANKI
KI

— MARDUKITE ZUISM —
A BRIEF INTRODUCTION*

According to the most ancient historical records written at the birth of our modern civilization...

432,000 years ago, a small population of advanced beings—called the <u>ANUNNAKI</u>—began developing the planet Earth for their purposes. These elite Self-Actualized spiritual beings resided on Earth in physical bodies, but found their forms inadequate for the physical labors required. Enter: the "Human Condition." Ancient "<u>cuneiform</u>" tablet writings from Sumerians and Babylonians of Mesopotamia are clear regarding the original creation and systematic programming of Humanity.

> <u>CUNEIFORM</u> is the oldest known writing system used by scribes of ancient Babylon to record their wisdom and the history of humanity on <u>clay tablets</u>.

"Cuneiform" is named for its style of wedge-shaped script formed by a <u>reed pen</u> called a "<u>stylus.</u>" Rather than an alphabet of letters, cuneiform writing is a system of "<u>signs</u>" representing "things" and "ideas." These may even be combined to represent even more complex "signs."

Many concepts adopted for modern "<u>Mardukite Zuism</u>" and its "<u>Systemology</u>" are derived from cuneiform tablets.

The ANUNNAKI introduced complex writing systems in order to program civilization and all parameters of Reality for the Human Condition. Legendary "<u>Tablets of Destiny</u>" (Divine Truth, supreme knowledge and cosmic power of the "gods") were first introduced to Humanity in the Babylonian narrative known best as the "<u>Epic of Creation.</u>

---

* "*Mardukite Zuism: A Brief Introduction*" Revised Version 2.0.

THE ARCANE TABLETS.

Ancient Babylonians used the *Tablets of Destiny & Creation Epic* to systematize all cosmic knowledge into a workable paradigm called "Mardukite Zuism"—a systemology received directly from the ANUNNAKI.

> PARADIGM : all-encompassing standard or religion used to view the world and communicate reality.
>
> SYSTEMOLOGY : applied philosophies (of *Mardukite Zuism*) combined with personal spiritual techniques and technology ("*Tech*") effectively demonstrating systematic principles of a "paradigm."

THE SYSTEMOLOGY OF LIFE, UNIVERSES & EVERYTHING.

The *Arcane Tablets* describe the division of the ALL by the LAW, outside of which is but INFINITY. The *Epic of Creation* describes these activities as "mythology." The "Standard Model of Systemology" that is applied to *Mardukite Zuism* uses the same information to demonstrate...

> that ALL ("AN-KI") envelops both:
> the Spiritual Existences ("AN")
> and the Physical Existences ("KI")
> divided by Cosmic Law and
> connected by Life-Awareness ("ZU")
> and beyond which is only the Abyss,
> an Infinity of Nothingness ("ABZU")

MARDUKITE ZUISM DEFINITIONS FOR STANDARD MODEL OF SYSTEMOLOGY.

> ABZU = the Abyss; Infinity; Infinity of Nothingness; that which extends, is exterior to and beyond of, all spiritual and physical existence.

ANKI : the ALL; All Existences; Everything that is AN and KI; Everything that is conceivable; represented by the "Standard Model of Systemology."

AN : the "Spiritual Universe" or "Heavenly Zone" comprised of spiritual energy-matter, in the direction of Infinity—the "Alpha" existence independent of, and superior to, the physical, *beta* or KI.

KI : the "Physical Universe" or "Earthly Zone" comprised of physical energy-matter in action across physical Space and observed as Time in the direction of Physical Continuity—"beta" existence condensed from, and subordinate to, the spiritual, *Alpha* or AN.

ZU L "to know"; "knowingness"; "Awareness" or "consciousness"; spiritual energy-matter of AN observed as "Lifeforce" in KI; "Spiritual Life Energy"; the actual personal spiritual beingness or "Awareness" of Self as the Alpha-Spirit which extends along a "line" from the Spiritual (AN) to the Physical (KI).

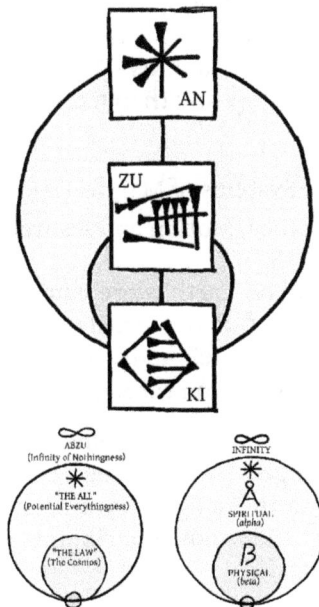

THE TABLETS OF DESTINY &
BABYLONIAN CREATION EPIC.

Seven cuneiform tablets compose the ancient _Babylonian Epic of Creation_, named the _Enuma Eliš_ by scholars after its opening lines. These seven tablets are the basis for what later traditions refer to as the "_Seven Days of Creation._" The _Epic of Creation_ tablets describe development of all existences with a Divine artistic perfection. The _Enuma Eliš_ is the core example of religious literature from Babylon, which served as the basis for ancient "_Mardukite Zuism_"—the first true systematized religion in history.

The Absolute _behind_ and _back of_ ALL Existence is referred to on the _Tablets of Destiny_ as the INFINITY OF NOTHINGNESS; a constant static latent unmanifest potentiality of ALL and Everythingness.

The LAW—Cosmic Law—is defined as the Cosmic Dragon—TIAMAT—on "_Epic of Creation_" Tablets. She is the First Cause or movement across a "Sea of Infinity." Later, the LAW becomes a division between Spiritual Existence (AN) and any Physical Universe (KI). The LAW—_Tiamat_—permeating ALL, uses the _Tablets of Destiny_ and then fixes the systems of finite potential:

The Systems of Manifestation—
Substance, Motion and Awareness.

"Before 'Heaven' or 'Earth' were named," a formation and interaction of active existences—"substances" and "bodies" and "Life" and "gods"—creates turbulence and waves of action through space.

The governing system of Cosmic Law—_Tiamat_—responds accordingly. She fixes the _Tablets of Destiny_ to her "deputy"—a messenger wave action of the LAW named "_Kingu_" and sends him rippling out to "meet" the _Anunnaki_ "gods."

The *Anunnaki Assembly* of "gods" prepare to battle The LAW. When none among them comes forth to engage, the *Anunnaki* "god" MARDUK volunteers as hero to confront *Kingu* and *Tiamat*—but with a condition that the *Anunnaki Assembly* recognize him as "Chief of the Gods" upon his success.

When *Marduk* approaches *Tiamat* (LAW) directly, he is flanked by *Kingu* and the "army of Ancient Ones." *Marduk* relinquishes the *Tablets of Destiny* from *Kingu*. With the *Tablets of Destiny*, *Marduk* successfully conquers the true understanding of "Cosmic Law" and thereby conquers *Tiamat*.

THE TABLETS OF DESTINY
& SELF-HONESTY.

Marduk uses the Tablets of Destiny to discover "<u>Self-Honesty</u>" and Divine Knowledge governing "<u>Cosmic Ordering</u>"— systems dividing the "Spiritual Universe" (AN) from a "Physical Universe" (KI).

The two Universe types are connected only by a stream of Spiritual Awareness (*Lifeforce*) that Sumerians called <u>ZU</u>.

Wisdom of the Arcane Tablets is later passed down to and concealed by an <u>ancient esoteric secret society</u> in Babylon: the Scribe-Magicians, High Priests and Priestesses of *Mardukite Zuism*.

<u>Self-Honesty</u> is a term describing an original "<u>Alpha</u>" state of <u>clear knowingness</u> and <u>Self-directed beingness</u>. "Self-Honesty" is the most basic and true expression of Self as "I-AM"—free of artificial attachments; reactive-response conditioning; and imposed or enforced programming as Reality for the Human Condition. Spiritual development in modern *Mardukite Zuism* is referred to as the "Pathway to Self-Honesty" and the "Gateway to Infinity." It is modeled directly from the Ancient Mystery Tradition as observed at the original Temples of Babylon.

KEYS TO THE GATEWAY

"I will take my Blood—and with Bone—I will fashion a
Race of Humans to keep Watch of the Gate. And from
the Blood of Kingu I will create another Race of Humans to inhabit the Earth in service to the Gods—so
shrines to the Anunnaki may be built and the temples
filled. I will bind the Elder Gods to the Watchtowers;
let them keep watch over the Gate of Abzu and the
Gate of Tiamat and Gate of Kingu—and with a Key
that shall be ever hidden, known to none, except only
to my Mardukites."

— MARDUK, *Enuma Eliš, Creation Tablet VI.*

THE ANUNNAKI LADDER OF LIGHTS &
BABYLONIAN GATEWAYS TO INFINITY.

ZIGGURAT TEMPLES in Babylonia—and throughout Mesopotamia—served to remind populations of the "bond" or ZU
connecting "Heaven" and "Earth." Seven-stepped "levels"
of the physical *Ziggurat Temples* of Babylonia—and seven
corresponding Gates—represent spiritual levels of actualized Awareness; states of Self-purification (or "spiritual
defragmentation") as they ascend in the direction of AN toward Infinity of Supreme Beingness—the Pathway of Self-
Honesty—in imitation of the footsteps of the gods during
their descent through the "spheres" or "Gates."

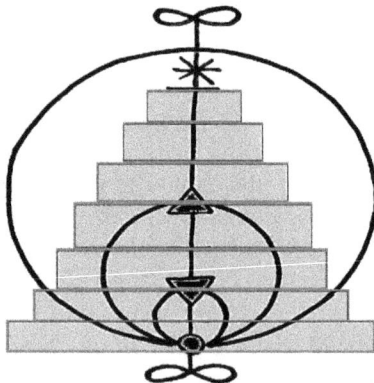

COSMOLOGY AND METAPHYSICS.

All Things in the Physical Universe are in motion—wave motions of "energy and matter in space measured as-and-across time." Continuity of the Physical Universe (KI) is divided by LAW and encompassed by the ALL (ANKI). The direction of AN extends toward ABZU, an Infinity of Nothingness beyond effective existence.

> The <u>Alpha Self</u> or <u>Alpha Spirit</u> is the true source—the "spiritual cause" of "physical effects." It engages <u>Self-determined WILL</u> from its "spiritual" <u>Alpha existence</u> as an Actualized Awareness impinging on "physical" <u>Beta existence</u> and experienced as "Life."

USING ANCIENT WISDOM TO UNLOCK HUMAN POTENTIAL.

Communication of clear wisdom and true knowledge from Arcane Tablets is distorted as it passes through time and geography, diverse languages and authoritarian cultures using the "Power" to program the masses and fragment the Human Condition away from Self-Honesty.

> Use of this ancient wisdom reveals the Keys to "<u>Cosmic Ordering</u>"—applying the highest understanding of "cause-and-effect" sequences to all action in the Physical Universe, and to all *Self-directed* applications of WILL-Intention and Effort.

MARDUKITE ZUISM, SYSTEMOLOGY & SPIRITUALITY.

The Spiritual Universe (AN)—of metaphysical or spiritual energy and metaphysical or spiritual matter is not dependent on the Physical Universe (KI) to exist; the two are existentially independent of each other, maintaining a single channel, conduit or connection, which is <u>Alpha Spirit</u> "Awareness" as Spiritual Life or ZU.

The Alpha Spirit engages a <u>ZU-line</u>, a spiritual lifeline of ZU energy to a genetic vehicle or organic body to experience physical beta existence.

MARDUKITE ZUISM DEFINITIONS FOR METAHUMAN SYSTEMOLOGY.

<u>ALPHA SPIRIT</u> : a Spiritual *life-form*; the True Self or "I-AM"; a unit of *Awareness;* a *Spiritual Beingness* that controls a physical body or "genetic vehicle" using a Lifeline or continuum of spiritual "ZU" energy.

<u>ASCENSION</u> : actualized Awareness elevated to (AN) spiritual existence that is exterior to beta-existence; the ability to *Self-direct* from *Spirit* as *Self* in existence independent of any "body."

<u>BETA-EXISTENCE</u> : manifestation of a Physical Universe (KI); conditions of energy-matter manifested in a state of condensed existence matching frequencies specific to space in the Physical Universe.

<u>FRAGMENTATION</u> : breaking apart; scattering the pieces; fractioning wholeness; fracture of holism; discontinuity; a separation of totality; anything outside or apart from original clarity (or *Self-Honesty*).

<u>GENETIC VEHICLE</u> : Physical *life-form*; physical (*beta*) body controlled by an Alpha Spirit using a continuous Lifeline of ZU energy; an organic catalyst for a Spirit to operate causes and observe effects (in *beta*).

<u>HUMAN CONDITION</u> : a standard issue default programmed state of Human experience; receptacle for Alpha Spirit Awareness that is generally accepted to be the extent of its potential identity (*Beingness*).

<u>ZU-LINE</u> : Spiritual Life-Energy (ZU) continuum; an energetic channel or Identity-Continuum connecting Alpha Spirit Awareness from Infinity-to-Infinity including the full Physical or *beta* range of existence.

THE HIGHEST FORM OF
TRUE DIVINE WORSHIP.

The true Destiny of Humanity is to achieve spiritual Self-Actualization; the reunion of Self with the Infinite.

Attaining Self-Honesty in this Life is the most important step a person can take toward achieving their highest ideals, goals and realizations as a Spiritual Being.

The Highest form of "True Worship" begins with the Spirit —the true Self—and all external practices, rituals, ceremonies and historical examples are but outer reflections of this ideal. The Highest form of "Sin" is against the Spirit— against the Self—and its ability to maintain Self-Honesty.

There are modes of thought, action and Self-direction of effort that will contribute toward Ascension; and modes that lead away from that.

Beta experiences of "Sin"—pain, fear, guilt, anger—are all related to personal fragmentation; and emotional turbulence from all of these may be released—and intention energy redirected—because:

We all co-create the reality we experience in this lifetime!

SPHERES OF EXISTENCE AND INFLUENCE &
A UTILITARIAN SYSTEMOLOGY OF ETHICS.

The prime directive of all beta existence is: *to exist*. The continuation of existence is the purpose behind all existence. Between realization of Self and Infinity, there are many spheres of existence that we may influence.

All of the spheres are interconnected. There is nothing in existence that is in absolute exclusion to all existence. Each sphere of existence supports subsequent existences and assists reaches toward higher spheres of influence.

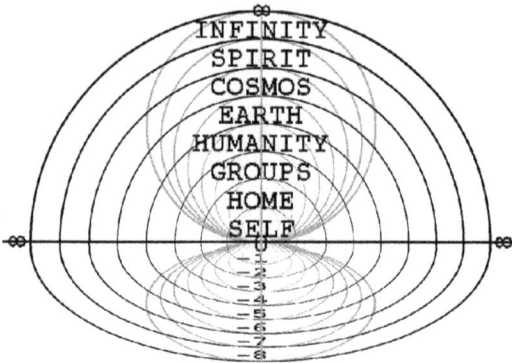

The greatest good contributes to the greatest continuation of optimum existence and survival for the greatest sphere of inclusion. Degrees of rightness and wrongness are determined by Cosmic Law and are reflected in the quality and continuation of optimal existence at the highest sphere of existence. Individual happiness is attained via the channel to the highest sphere. Unhappiness is a result of "selfishness," lack of "Spiritual Self-Actualization" and/or reach of "Actualized Awareness" beyond *Self* as identified to a *body*.

ZU : MARDUKITE ZUISM & MODERN ZUIST RELIGION.

History demonstrates how dangerous, troublesome and easily misused the concept of "RELGION" is; so, for purposes of incorporating *Mardukite Zuism* and its *Systemology* as a contemporary standard, the idea is treated here as defined.

> RELIGION : a concise spiritual paradigm, fixed set of beliefs and practices, regarding Divinity, Infinite Beingness—or else "God."

—*Mardukite Zuism* operates under a premise of very specific beliefs and "systemology" of "applied spiritual technology."

—*Mardukite Zuist Religious Doctrine* fundamentally relays the previously described "Highest forms" of Worship, Cosmic Law, and Ethics.

Mardukite Zuist Spiritual Doctrines and its *Systemology* successfully meet modern "religious" criteria for:

a) A Description of Cosmic Creation;

b) Belief in a Supreme Infinite Being;

c) Ethics Leading to Human Ascension;

d) Ethics of Conduct Toward all Life and Existence;

e) Immortality of the Human Spirit;

f) A Published Library of Religious Literature;

g) Traditions of Practice and Application; and

h) A Spiritual Advisement Methodology.

GOALS & IDEALS OF MARDUKITE ZUISM.

The word "ZU" meant "knowing" in original Sumerian cuneiform script. Goals and ideals of Zuism reflect this. *Mardukite Zuism & Systemology* seeks to assist an individual in reclaiming a total realization of the True Self or "I-AM" knowingly as the Immortal Alpha Spirit, in line with a most ancient directive: to "Know Thyself."

In view of the fact that all modern humans are subjected to technologies depriving them of their freedoms to *be, think, know* and pursue truth: goals and ideals of *Mardukite Zuism & Systemology* are to effectively repair abilities and elevate certainty of an Individual to increase and direct "Actualized Awareness" toward Higher Gateways of Spiritual Ascension.

INFINITY, "GOD" & SUPREME BEINGNESS

Spiritual Philosophy of *Mardukite Zuism* is systematized by a Standard Model of Systemology. It demonstrates Absolute Supreme Beingness associated with the Highest realization of "God" as INFINITY. No thing is Higher or Absolute than the *Infinity of Nothingness*—and reducing Supreme Beingness to any finite personality or character trait is to limit and defile what is herewith represented, but with lesser "words" and mundane sentiments or semantics.

> The Highest Name of God cannot be conceived
> —hence our symbolic use of the Infinity Sign:
>
> ∞
>
> ...or Sumerian cuneiform word-sign: "ABZU"—
> "The Infinite Nothingness and Source of All ZU."

—The Spiritual Universe (AN) is *All-as-One* because it exists as an infinite singularity or stasis: infinite potential with no gradient or observed motion; which is its own continuity.

—The Physical Universe (KI) is *All-as-One* because it is in continuous motion, with all manifest parts working systematically as the condensed solid continuity of beta-existence.

—A "spiritual continuum" or "conduit channel" of ZU (or a "*Zu-line*") from a Spiritual Universe (AN)—links our Awareness levels of "I-AM," "True Self" or Spirit ("Alpha Spirit") with varying potential "Point-of-View" and degrees of motion experienced in the Physical Universe.

—The Alpha Spirit or "Soul" is the true Awareness, "I" or "Self" connected to the operation and control of the physical body.

BASIC CONCEPT OF THE HUMAN SPIRIT.

> The true Self is the "I" or "I-AM" or "Spirit"
> regardless of its *perceived* position in spaces,
> *Point-of-View*, degree or level of Awareness.
> Spirit remains at its original fixed true point.

Whatever "spiritual energy-matter" (*if any*) that may compose the Alpha Spirit or makeup of "soul"—it must occupy this "other space" with its spiritual existence and then project its Awareness and Will onto the Physical Universe (KI) in order to experience the *Game* we call "*Life.*"

This "*Spiritual Life Energy*" or *Awareness* of a *Spiritual Being* is treated as a "Lifeforce" and "Consciousness" and goes by many names throughout the history of language, mysticism and spirituality—but we find the idea first treated as <u>ZU</u> on cuneiform tablets of Mesopotamia.

> On an Identity-lifeline or continuum of ZU energy, an Alpha Spirits is operating from a Spiritual Universe to experience in *beta-existence*. We refer to this concept as the "*<u>ZU-line</u>*" on the Standard Model of Systemology to illustrate the projected Awareness from Spirit (as an epicenter or fixed point) to any other *Point-of-view* (POV) anywhere in existence.

ZU is the name given to the spiritual beingness or essence of all Life in existence—and Self is a concentrated center or focal point that projects Awareness on a ZU-continuum or Zu-line toward a point of artificial Identity separate from Self.

The True Self of an Individual Human is a "spiritual universe cause" of "physical universe effects"—engaging as an immortal Alpha Spirit with a Self-determined Will actualized as an Awareness along a ZU-continuum (or "*Zu-line*"), extending from Infinity-to-Infinity, through every possible frequency and vibration along the total spectrum of physical and metaphysical existence.

THE SYSTEMOLOGY OF SPIRITUAL ADVISEMENT COUNSELING PRACTICES FOR MARDUKITE ZUISM

The Mardukite Chamberlains, an underground research organization established in 2009, dedicated itself to recovery and consolidation of relevant historical, scriptural & ritual records of ancient Mardukite Babylon in Mesopotamia, following up the founding of Mardukite Ministries (Mardukite Zuism) by Joshua Free the previous year, in 2008.

By 2011, a Mardukite Alumni faction (International Systemology Society) began research and development into new methods of:

> applying ancient wisdom as a futurist spiritual technology
> that effectively awakens, unlocks and fully actualizes
> spiritual potential of the Human Condition.

A systematic and logical approach to spirituality is visibly demonstrable on the Standard Model of Systemology, where ZU-line frequencies are represented at various degrees:

- "zero-point" body death;
- cellular life and sensory perceptions of a genetic body;
- bio-chemicals induced by emotion;
- thoughts and intention transmitted between our Alpha Spirit and the "genetic vehicle"—
- all the way "up" the scale to a perfected clarity of Self-Actualized Awareness of I-AM as our true "Alpha" state, just below Infinity and Absolute Beingness.

Full potential of ZU in is only altered from its natural state as a result of personal fragmentation of the Human Condition. This may be restored by systematic spiritual practices.

The *Pathway to Self-Honesty* is a personal journey and spiritual adventure marked by progressive clearing of personal energy channels fragmented by emotional imprinting and programming-data accumulated from "experiences" in the environment—the "debris" that fragments the total actualized experience of Self in Awareness as the Alpha Spirit.

The first and most important step—Before an individual can actualize potentials of the Spirit as Self, they must fully realize:

> The *I-AM Self* and the *Alpha Spirit* are One and the same.
> This state of Knowingness is a primary intention of basic
> spiritual practices of Mardukite Zuism & Systemology.

Mardukite Zuism books and *Systemology* advanced training courses are available to Mardukite Ministers seeking qualification as specialized Instructors, Clergy, Priests, Priestess, and/or Professional Pilots of systematic processing.

DISCOVERY OF SPIRITUAL LIFE ENERGY & THE SUMERIAN CONCEPT OF "ZU" THE ORIGINAL 2019 EDITION FOREWORD

by Reed Penn

We are standing now at the cusp of a true "New Age" for humanity—standing in witness to the very first tears of light on the horizon of the Crystal Dawn. Sparks of clear light from a forthcoming Crystal Age peek out to awaken the first *seeds* and *cells* on Earth to a new realization, signaling the inception of a *Coming Race*,[*] one that undeniably represents Human Destiny: the evolutionary future of the Human Condition. This future may be shaped in Self-Honesty only by the highest caliber *"spiritual technologies"* at our disposal—methods that only a small esoteric demographic of the population has kept a possession of, and which is markedly only being developed, refined and *radiated* into this existence by those few who are "in the *know*."

Evident that our society is fast approaching a glass ceiling is everywhere—limitation of the Human Condition fixed solely to external technologies, low degrees of Awareness and faulty education; all of which have led our present state of the Human Condition toward its inevitable zero point. And the mantra that seems to be rising up from the underground voices is unmistakable: *"Evolve or die."* At every turn of our attention we are faced with more and more problems resulting from grievous errors long past by previous generations—and *their* vision of truth. When does the old cycle end? Where are the new solutions? How do we arrive at the next evolution of Humanity and the unfoldment of its latent potentials buried within? When do *we* rise up in acceptance of our own spiritual destiny and become worthy receptacles "in the *kNow*"?

---

[*] A reference to Edward Bulwer-Lytton's 1871 novel: *"Vril, the Power of the Coming Race"* (and origins for *"Vril"* concept).

Mardukite Zuism—and its applied spiritual philosophy known as *Systemology**—has appeared now on the scene for the 21st century, very literally, to provide the *map* to *that* "*know.*" Joshua Free has pointedly demonstrated this—with *crystal clarity*—throughout various texts providing a brand new Esoteric Research Library to support the "*Mardukite Systemology*" and "*Mardukite Zuist*" paradigm.

Nearly a decade in the making behind the scenes—since the first materials composing "<u>*Systemology: The Original Thesis*</u>" were issued in 2010 and 2011—Joshua Free recently presented a synthesis of the complete fundamentals of *Mardukite Systemology* and its direct application to the emotional range of "ZU" energy, in the paramount textbook "<u>*The Tablets of Destiny: Using Ancient Wisdom to Unlock Human Potential.*</u>" The second installment of the textbook was released publically a month later, demonstrating methods of releasing hidden stores of our personal "ZU" energy at higher intellectual levels, as originally developed for an intensive course that was once only available directly (and in person) from the Mardukite Systemology Office: "<u>*Crystal Clear: The Self-Actualization Manual & Guide to Total Awareness.*</u>"

This present volume—"<u>*The Power of ZU*</u>"—treats the Systemology of the Human Condition from a different approach than previously described, meaning: as applied directly to the physical world; to the physical state of reality; and ultimately, to the physical nature of the organic "*Genetic Vehicle*" (or "body") that our *Alpha Spirit* commands in order to experience this "*physical reality*" on Earth—the "physical zone" that Sumerians called "KI" in their cuneiform tablet literature. As a holistic approach toward an increase of *Awareness* and pathway of spiritual evolution, the field of Systemology must necessarily not slight out the most obvious effects and applications that the esoteric wisdom from the Ancient Mystery School directly has to offer toward our most "material" elements of Life and *livingness* during this present "occupation" or "control" of the Human Condition.

---

* Also *NexGen Systemology* or *Mardukite Systemology*, &tc.

Combined *Awareness* as it applies to all levels of "ZU" radiating from the Human Condition—physical, emotional, intellectual, spiritual—is what provides a *Seeker* with the most effective tools to reclaim lost enthusiasm and certainty about *Life*; unwind and release forgotten stores of vital energy; reprogram fragmented thought patterns and unproductive behavioral cycles that assist to promote good health and physical well-being; to be more productive and efficient in material efforts; and quite simply, to unfold the *knowingness* inherent in the freedom of the spirit—the true "I-AM" or "*Alpha Spirit*" that is directing and controlling the *Awareness* of all experience as Reality. The way ahead is cleared. Open the Gates of Understanding and make your journey Home on the *Pathway to Self-Honesty*.

Δ Δ Δ Δ Δ Δ Δ

I originally wrote this article—my one frugal contribution toward *Mardukite Zuism* and *NexGen Systemology*—to supply a *Foreword* to Joshua Free's "*Tablets of Destiny*" (*Liber-One*).

I was asked, at that time, to apply my research and experience as a long-standing "*Mardukite Systemologist*"—a phrase that perhaps has only now earned some wider meaning on account of the most recent developmental literary efforts by Joshua Free. In that portion of the article (given in *Liber-One*), I focused primarily on geographic, historical and *systemological* background information necessary to introduce what the author presented within "*Tablets of Destiny*."

The extent of what I provided in the "linguistic analysis" portion was cut short—and only the part distinguishing true meaning behind semantics of "*Fate*" and "*Destiny*" was included. Little did I know at the time, but the second half of my article (primarily emphasizing meaning of "ZU"), which did not see print in *that* edition, was held back so it could be reworked to introduce a completely separate title—the volume you are in possession of now: "*The Power of ZU*."

The word "ZU" has received more significant attention in certain circles this past decade—where in the former decade, it seemed that "ANUNNAKI" was on everyone's word-of-the-day toilet-paper. But, having formerly settled the matter of "ANUNNAKI" in the *Mardukite Core,** the present scope for *Mardukite Systemology*—and foundations of *Mardukite Zuism*—is mostly rooted in the utmost understanding of what is referred to as "ZU" on the *Arcane Tablets* of Mesopotamian origin. Certainly, this same concept may be actually found, referred to by various names, in back of most ancient spiritual traditions—and even the more effective modern metaphysical methodologies—but we are treating the subject as "ZU" as directly referred to in the spiritual texts of *Mardukite Zuism* (ancient and modern), based on its appearance in a Sumerian vocabulary that predates any other known properly written languages.

We find many interesting concepts and ideograms retained from pre-Babylonian (Sumerian) uses of cuneiform—certain Sumerian words continued to be found directly in later periods, even after the common or native language had changed abruptly in more elaborate or refined forms of cuneiform-represented language (in this case a shift to Babylo-Akkadian from the former Sumerian). The *Mardukite Zuists*, presently represented strongest in *North America*, are not the only portion of the Human population that has identified very strongly with the concept of "ZU" or a religio-spiritual philosophy to be appropriately called "*Zuism.*" This subject has also been taken up in several countries, and by groups operating independently of the *Mardukite Office.* In might therefore seem appropriate—for all those persons concerned—that we treat very seriously the simple question: "*What is ZU?*"

---

* Texts of the Mardukite Esoteric Research Library published by the Joshua Free Imprint, such as *"Complete Anunnaki Bible" "Sumerian Religion" "Babylonian Myth & Magic"* and *"The Complete Book of Marduk by Nabu"*—all of which (and others) are combined in the Grade-II Master Edition anthology: *"Necronomicon: The Complete Anunnaki Legacy."*

Joshua Free provides a strong basis and inertia for present and future developments of *Mardukite Zuism* and *Mardukite Systemology* in his first true volume on the subject, "*Tablets of Destiny*"—upon which the methodology was extended to further considerations for "*Crystal Clear.*" This second book was originally intended as a "part two" of the same volume —separated due to the sheer length and the author's desire to further refine "*Crystal Clear*" as a Self-guided course text-book; even expanded to include three additional transcripts from lectures privately given in October 2019 to members of the *Systemology Society*.

But perhaps the most solid and concise launch point for this discussion is the precise summation provided in the most recently released booklet: "*Mardukite Zuism: A Brief Introduction*"*—it is from this, the author's own precise language, that we are able to establish a sure-footed idea to support a solid conceptual understanding of "*ZU.*"

Δ Δ Δ Δ Δ Δ Δ

Mardukite Systemology is based on an expert *systematization* of ancient wisdom into lore that we now call the "Standard Model"—or else the "Mardukite Standard ZU Model of Systemology" and a host of other names. It demonstrates an interconnectivity between *Infinity* at one end of a con-tinuum with *Infinity* at the other end, and through each and every spectrum between and all levels and layers and de-grees of potential existence. This very continuum of interconnectedness is referred to as the "ZU-line" in mod-ern literature and spiritual philosophies of *Mardukite Zuism* and *Mardukite Systemology*.

It would, in fact, be quite difficult to fully appreciate the "Standard Model" of *Mardukite Systemology*—or effectively apply any of its philosophies and spiritual technologies—without first having a better understanding of this word we have begun tossing around—"*ZU.*"

---

* Included previously in this present edition of "*Power of Zu.*"

This concept of "ZU"—and the systematization of the same—is by no means an artificial concoction born from the imagination of Joshua Free; but it is based on the concise intellectual and spiritual observations *radiated* from the author.

It is incredible to see concrete published forms of this work finally arriving—such as "*Tablets of Destiny*" and "*Crystal Clear*."There are a few of us that have been privy to more of these happenings behind-the-scenes; some of us are more aware of the years of intensive, but silent, underground research supporting it—not to mention Joshua Free's unique style of "use-it-if-you-can; take-it-or-leave it" experimentation at the *Mardukite Office* and *Systemology Society*. In the end, the "Mardukite Standard ZU-Model of Systemology" was refined for seven years until it could establish the basic premise of applied spiritual philosophy for *Mardukite Zuism*:

> "...that the ALL ('AN-KI') envelops both the *Spiritual Existences* ('AN') and the *Physical Existences* ('KI'), which are divided by COSMIC LAW and connected by *Life-Awareness* ('ZU'); beyond which is only the ABYSS ('AB-ZU'), an *Infinity of Nothingness*. The *Arcane Tablets* are very clear in their descriptions of a 'division' of the ALL by the LAW—outside of which is but INFINITY; and the ancient Babylonian Epic of Creation describes the same model of activity, but in 'mythological' terms."[*]

If we are to be absolutely precise in our semantic analysis: the word "ZU" appears twice above in reference to specifically Sumerian-Babylonian language concepts (or ideogram signs). Yes, it appears directly on its own: "*Life-Awareness* ('ZU')"—but it is included in another significant concept; one that is unavoidable when dealing with *Mardukite Zuism/ Systemology* philosophies, or even the subject of Mesopotamian cosmology in general, and that is the "ABYSS ('AB-ZU'), an *Infinity of Nothingness*."

---

[*] Excerpting *"Mardukite Zuism—Brief Introduction"* given previously.

The subject of "ABZU" has eluded most scholars and even many esoteric mystics that are unable to fully appreciate the magnitude of what an *"Infinity of Nothingness"* truly is—of which Joshua Free explores quite deeply in previous volumes.

"Infinite Latent Potential" is not an academic subject that is often explored—but it is represented in lore quite clearly as an "Infinite Source"—the "Father" and "Heart" of "ZU" outside the domain of anything that may be conceived from the individuated consciousness or *Awareness* of "Self." Even as our true "Alpha Spirit" nature, Joshua Free expresses how we are an individual wave-crest of a sea that otherwise spreads out without variation or interruption Infinitely as One in all directions—and none. But this, in itself, does not fully describe the personal nature of ZU as "Spiritual Energy" providing our very *Lifeforce* or *Awareness*.

> We have now, for our *Systemology*,
> this new classification of "ZU"
> quite simply as *"Awareness."*

I say "simply," and yet it is milestones ahead of any former realizations on the subject—and there have been more than a few persons in the past that have attempted to tackle the overwhelming task of transliterating, translating and/or interpreting the cuneiform script recorded on these ancient tablets. It became clear to early *Mardukite* researchers and *Systemologists* that meanings (or semantics) from this ancient well-springs may be carried in every which direction. We find this even in the words we more easily recognize and use today in our vocabulary. What then do we expect to find from words and ideas radiated in messages that are thousands of years old, using languages that have long since been erased from memory? It is such an effort that has allowed the concept of "ZU" to now define a larger scope of understanding than what literal definitions for it commonly carry—or are interpreted to carry.

According to modern lexicons by scholarly linguists and scholars (many that still inappropriately refer to their archaeological science as "Assyriology"),

> the Sumerian word-sign *ZU* is a verb,
> meaning "*to know*," or else "*knowing*."

It is meant to distinguish a type of "true knowledge" or "true learning" that an individual has acquired; literally *to be* in "*the know*." The applications to older Sumerian literature vary greatly—but the ambiguity is found to dissipate by the time of Mardukite Babylon and systematic refinement of language, tradition and culture in ancient Mesopotamia.

Akkadian language—as used in "Old Babylon"—now included other words to represent "learning" (*lamadu*) and "scientific knowledge" (*edu* or *idu*). During the same time, certain former Sumerian expressions were retained to represent the highest ideals of "Divine Knowledge" as they were first recorded in Sumerian. This includes the expression of "ZU"—of which we are no longer concerned with confusing it with an "activity" of *learning* and *knowing*, but now treated as an essence of the same; the very essence and highest archetypal realization of *learning* and *knowing* as it applies to the Human Condition: "*Awareness.*"

It is the essence of "*Actualized Awareness*" that Joshua Free refers to when incorporating this ancient concept into modern *Mardukite Zuism*, and especially *Mardukite Systemology*. Without the firm establishment of the "Standard Model" and its definitions—including "ZU"—the latest developments of *Systemology* as an applied spiritual technology would not be nearly as effective or workable as they were discovered to be, although it should be made clear that many of the realizations were not reached "overnight," but over a long period of time that required "practical experimentation" to determine what would yield the necessary results and what would be flushed out of the final refinement of our own methodology.

Although greatly enhanced by the understanding presented in the newly developed volumes—such as "_Tablets of Destiny_" and "_Crystal Clear_"—this present work is based on notebooks kept immediately following the period when discourses for "_The Original Thesis_" were originally released. Many _Seekers_ that are just now discovering such publications may not be aware that such developments were expected by some individuals for nearly a decade, while the author spent considerable time behind-the-scenes in their refinement and to "wait when the stars were right" for its dissemination around the world.

Δ Δ Δ Δ Δ Δ Δ

Around the same time that discourses for "_The Original Thesis_" were completed, Joshua Free began to develop an "alternate route" that could bridge the _Mardukite Grade_ of material to the vision that he held for a futurist _Mardukite Zuist Systemology_—and the concept of "_Moroii ad Vitam_"‡ emerged in immediate response to cultural themes and requests by _Seekers_ at that time. It held a similar premise, but more elementary and pop-New Age. It became a resting point, since most _Seekers_ graduating the "_Mardukite_" Grade then—and those just discovering the _Mardukite_ paradigm— were not at all "ready" to take on full ramifications of what the real intended "_NexGen Systemology_" was about.

As a result, further developments—such as "_Tablets of Destiny_" or "_Crystal Clear_" and public presentation of "_Mardukite Zuism_"—were held back until recently; at the cusp of the new decade, from which we can expect to see a great deal to happen. Meanwhile, other spiritual and religious groups around the world—taking interest in ancient Mesopotamian studies—have begun to spring up; but among the forefront of these, those witnessing long-standing efforts toward this realization, will continue to recognize the paramount contributions from Joshua Free as a bridge to these ends.

---

‡   See _"Vampyre's Handbook: The Secret Rites of Modern Vampires"_
    10th Anniversary Collector's Edition by Joshua Free.

Joshua Free completed materials for "*Moroii ad Vitam*" in 2015, then returned attentions exclusively to the private development of "*Mardukite Systemology*"—outside public view with the "*Systemology Society.*" *This* effort continues today. It was actually quite obvious to some of us just how much *Systemology* was already incorporated into Mardukite material along the way—but particularly in "*Moroii ad Vitam*," which really only served as a way-station or rest stop while any work beyond "<u>*Systemology: The Original Thesis*</u>" still waited to appear.

> But, many long-time readers will notice that appearances of *Systemology*—mostly indirectly—have steadily increased in the authors work since the 1990's.

Something else was also happening in 2015, albeit mostly unnoticed except for a few of us nerds in the academic world: Jared Norris Wolfe, studying at the University of California (UCLA), produced a thesis paper (readily available from the university) titled: "<u>*ZU: The Life of a Sumerian Verb in Early Mesopotamia*</u>." This obscure thesis provided, at the very least, some further substance to the conceptual pursuit of modern "Zuism" as a paradigm set apart from *other* typical ways of looking at or experiencing Reality.

> For although *Mardukite Zuism* and *Mardukite Systemology* stretch in their range to include all of what we might consider *universalism*, the originating point of observation for the *Mardukites* has always emphasized data involving the "inception of the systems" and "programming of the Human Condition" as it appears in ancient Mesopotamia.

Wolfe's paper contributes, very succinctly, the "epistemological and practical implications associated with the concept of '*knowing*' in Mesopotamian texts," especially given that at that time there were "no other systematic lexical discussions of the verbal root meaning '*to know*'" in existence."

The subject remains something of an ambiguous conception between modern revivals; there are *other* groups and factions that retain more literal applications of this expression: to mean literally *"knowing"*—as in the esoteric or spiritual education of an individual, but the Mardukites have already referred to this type of apprenticeship in another context: the Akkadian word *"edu"* or *"idu"*—a word derived from the name for the original Mesopotamian storehouse of "Divine Knowledge" kept by the Anunnaki god ENKI at his private city of *"Eridu."* This is cited frequently in Mardukite mythographics: concerning the "science laboratory" of ENKI; the apprenticeship of MARDUK as the "Magician" and eventually NABU as "High Priest"—all of which take place in prehistoric *"Eridu"*—an education linked directly with the *"Tablets of Destiny"* and Divine "ME" originally kept there.[*]

In the thesis by Jared Wolfe, Sumerian and Akkadian applications of "ZU" (as *"to know"*) are explored in a manner we might expect from the academic world—and outside of *Mardukite Zuism* and *NexGen Systemology*—which is to say phrasic examples of *"to know"* in vocabulary, but mainly restricted to expressions regarding *"having"* or being in "possession of knowledge." Yet, we see that the higher ideals are not completely slighted out of usage for this term, when Wolfe states:—

> "the most subjective accusative is to be found in the ancient but well-known injunction *to know thyself.*"

This is the concept of *"knowing"* that is demonstrated specifically in *Mardukite Zuism* and *Mardukite Systemology* without argument. As explained in lectures by Joshua Free, this state of *"knowingness"* carries a quality—or requires a qualification—that is beyond or above *"havingness"* since: to "not know" is to "not have."

---

[*] See *"Tablets of Destiny"* by Joshua Free.

On the other hand, a thesis paper, particularly one written by a student classically "educated" or "learned"—and is perhaps applying some epistemological self-help in validating his own "education" or "learning"—might tend to focus on what is referred to in *Systemology* as "*beta-Awareness*," or else what is accessible concerning the rigidly fixed range of the Human Condition as "physical perception."

Mardukite Systemology does not disqualify "knowing accessed by the senses," except to the degree that it is *fragmented,* which is to say not able to be experienced outside of other predisposed or pre-programmed influences or *facets.* Sensory knowledge is often too easily conditioned to be reliable; and it operates off of physical-body sensors that a *Spirit* is relying on to "do the looking for them" as is talked about in some of the advanced courses.

It is clearly demonstrated in other recent materials composing *Mardukite Systemology* that traditional "gut-instincts" or similar "reactions" are primarily *conditioned* responses that must be *defragmented* if a person is to effectively access the highest true innate spiritual faculties called "intuition," which is itself yet another ideal archetype of "*knowing.*" It is to this higher form of *knowing* and the *spiritual essence* of *Awareness* that is referred to as <u>ZU</u> within the present volume and all throughout the related materials.

In *Mardukite Systemology*, we consider all of the faculties attached to the ZU-line of a personal Identity—which is to say the *Lifeline* that connects the *Identity* as *Awareness* from its point of spiritual fragmentation (away from the ABZU) and all down through the levels of condensation that result in *Awareness* and *control* of a physical/organic body as a "genetic vehicle" for experiencing the Physical Universe.

When one considers all of the faculties involved in processing experience—whether to recall a memory, to direct attention and distinguish, to analyze, to consider (all of which are treated directly in "<u>*Crystal Clear*</u>")—these all relate to the certainty of one's own *knowing*, which in Systemology is directly regarded as the "level" of *Awareness* that is being maintained. Such then distinguishes an equal level of appreciable "understanding" or "knowledge" that is marked by varied degrees of fragmentation, personal programming, emotional encoding and so forth—all of which are demonstrated clearly in the previously mentioned processing textbooks on *Mardukite Systemology*.

Δ Δ Δ Δ Δ Δ Δ

A literal concept of "ZU" has been most recently defined by Joshua Free for *Mardukite Zuism:*—

"ZU = 'to know'; 'knowingness'; 'Awareness' or 'consciousness'; a concentration of spiritual energy and spiritual matter (of 'AN') that is observed as 'Lifeforce' (in 'KI'); 'Spiritual Life Energy'; the essence of a personal spiritual Identity or 'Awareness' of Self as Spirit, which extends alone a 'line' from the Spiritual Universe ('AN') to the Physical Universe ('KI')."*

Another of the interesting philosophical suggestions put forth by Joshua Free during the course of establishing any set *logic* to apply to these new spiritual technologies, which is not otherwise reflected in the sciences and humanities taught today:

—————————
* Excerpting *"Mardukite Zuism—Brief Introduction"* given previously.

> "*Life*—as we understand it in *beta-existence*—does not 'become' Aware; *Awareness* is the *I-AM* that is back of all *Life*. Each and every physical cell carries an amount of *consciousness activity*, which is *Awareness*; and every cell is in possession of a perspective for a *Self* in *Awareness* as *I-AM*."[‡]

Presently—in *Mardukite Systemology*—we are now in possession of this Sumerian-cuneiform ideogram (and ideology) for *Awareness-of-Awareness*—or *Awareness-of-Self-Knowingness*—as our highest archetype for the concept of an "Alpha Spirit" (or at least its composure) in history.

For our purposes "ZU" is not necessarily linguistically related to "knowledge" and "knowing" on a sensory level, but rather as the means or essence of the *Self* that is "in the know" and the quality and quantity of this objectively being considered as *Awareness* in *Mardukite Systemology*. On the original cuneiform version of the "Standard Model" we find the position of "ZU" (as "*knowingness*") as a connecting line between two other "spheres" or "states" of positive or active "ZU" distinguished as Physical/"KI" (or "*havingness*") and Spiritual Heights/"AN" (or "*Beingness*").

For example—as will be already understood by experienced *Mardukite Systemologists*: each of the following describes the same ZU-line across the Standard Model:—

-8 ← (0/KI) "Havingness" ↔ "Knowingness" ↔ "Beingness" (AN)
(-8 or *Infinity*) ← (0.0) ← My / Cycles of Action / I → (8 or *Infinity*)
ABZU -8 ← 0 ← My Body ↔ My Self/My ↔ I-AM ↔ I → 8 ABZU

Δ Δ Δ Δ Δ Δ

There is a linguistic connection between the "Z" and the "S" in all ancient etymologies. Therefore, we should not be surprised to find a direct link between the Sumerian signs for "ZU" and "SU"—and there most certainly in one. In fact, the

---

‡   Paraphrasing one of the original *"Power of ZU"* lectures.

two expressions are represented by an almost identical sign with one exception: an additional horizontal bar is found enclosed within the "SU" sign. This connection is not arbitrary, nor is an examination of the same. Basic meaning of the signs are understood simply by classifying origins for it: a *basin* or *cistern* that is to house or hold the waters or "volume" that is treated as "knowledge" and "experience." The metaphor of a "glass" or "cup" filled with such "knowledge" and "experience" is actually literal for the purposes of an ancient Sumerian cuneiform sign to represent it. But, much like what we are witness to regarding interpretations supplied by Joshua Free, the "ZU" itself is akin to the idea of "capacity" and the "SU" is what it is filled with.

The two concepts of "ZU" and "SU" blur together as vaguely in the technical interpretations we are given by scholars of ancient tablets, just as much as these concepts are only vaguely understood and differentiated by the common population today. The same can be said for the distinction between "*Fate*" and "*Destiny*"—an explanation of which was supplied in the Foreword to "*Tablets of Destiny.*"

The concept of "ZU" and its semantic combination with "SU" enters into exclusive esoteric use in Babylon around 2100 B.C. and the inception of the original Mardukite Babylonians. In this respect, Joshua Free—who is otherwise known for an emphasis on purely "Babylonian" semantics—has decided to incorporate the word "ZU" as a symbol of the highest ideal discernible, or else the "archetype" for a concept that should not otherwise be reduced to a "common-language understanding." This occurs many times throughout history where a successive culture would retain the language and terminology of an earlier one for exclusively "sacred" purposes. It is my understanding that this was the original intention behind an emphasis on "ZU" and "*Zuism*" as a much needed distinction or regard for the applied spiritual technology that is being developed and/or that which is already evident within the basic framework (or literally "systemology") of "*Mardukite Zuism.*"

The "Standard Model" and "ZU-line" developed by Joshua Free is now a staple of modern *Mardukite Zuism* and its *Systemology*, though it is based very literally and directly upon the "BAB.ILU" (or "BAB.ILI") methodology of the Mardukite Chamberlains introduced in Grade-II material—such as "*The Complete Anunnaki Bible*" "*Sumerian Religion*" and "*Babylonian Myth & Magic.*"

It has become quite evident that *Truth* is unchanging—whatever *It* actually *Is*, independent of us—and yet our interaction with *Truth*, our actualized ability to contain the *Truth*, is entirely subject to who and what we choose *to be* as its receptacle.

> A *Seeker* that actually does come to "realizations" intended by the *processes* and *methodology* present within the total scope of *Mardukite Zuism* and *Mardukite Systemology* will very coyly be at the highest levels of the ancient *Priests* and *Priestesses*, *Mystics* and *Gatekeepers*—all of which appear to have retained an "esoteric" understanding of *Life*, *Reality* and the *Universe* that was independent and "hermetically-sealed" away from the "exoteric" public scrutiny of the common population masses.[*]

This division of "accessibility" has, until quite recently, always been in place—and it is the equal dispersion of these mysteries to all, presently undertaken by Joshua Free, that makes the *Mardukite Path* truly stand apart in the 21st Century from all that came before; which is quite considerable.

The concept of the former Sumerian "ZU" being secreted away—the entire Sumerian language being occulted by later Babylonian developments of Akkadian and Assyrian—we find that the Orders of Priests, Priestesses and Scribes first occupying the Mardukite Temples, refer to their Pathway as "being in the footsteps of the gods" (or Divine), as expressed by Kyra Kaos in contributory revisions to the "*Mardukite*

---

[*] See Joshua Free's edition of *Pantheisticon* by John Toland.

Zuism: A Brief Introduction" booklet. What is perhaps not so well known is that the ancient axiom or motto held by the esoteric Nabu-Scribes, Priests and Priestesses in charge of intellectual and spiritual administration was:

"_i-la-da-ha-at_" / "_ilu-da-ha-at_" :: God is True Knowledge
"_ia-da-ah-ta-D-_" / "_ia-da-ah-ta-Dingir_" :: True Knowledge is God

We could of course, substitute the Babylonian "_(i)da_" here for "_Awareness._" Joshua Free believes that this sentiment was naturally retained verbatim from the original "Ancient Mystery School" of Mesopotamian prehistory, "_Eridu_"—the place where systematized sciences and learning began for the modern cycle of civilization on planet Earth, under the instruction of ENKI. Dispersal of this "legacy" is very clearly described on the ancient tablets—some of which is quite succinctly paraphrased in the "_Tablets of Destiny_" textbook.

All of this background is intended to provide the new or returning reader with a historical and practical introduction to the very concept of "ZU" and the application of the word in Mardukite literature as the very spiritual-life-essence of "consciousness" that we may consider with the highest ideal or idea of the concept of "_Awareness._" Without such an understanding, the repeated use of these words throughout _Mardukite Systemology_ literature—and the full scope of _Mardukite Zuism_—will not render a communication relay of appropriate meaning. The words will just be words. And isn't that an interesting irony for our purposes?—Since it is these very types of fragmentation that we are now seeking to overcome for the Human Condition in Systemology.

Δ Δ Δ Δ Δ Δ Δ

The scope of the present volume—"_The Power of ZU_"—delivers an understanding of "ZU" as recorded and understood for the "_Systemology Society_" from 2013 through 2018. This means after "_Systemology: The Original Thesis,_" but prior to the formal release of the _Grade-III_ materials of "_Mardukite_

Systemology"—such as "*The Tablets of Destiny*" and "*Crystal Clear*"—that have gone on to directly advance upon the ancient wisdom uncovered during the initial (*Grade II*) work of the "*Mardukite Chamberlains*" (conducted between 2009 and 2012) for the "*Mardukite Core*" *Research Library*. A combination of both these "Grades" constitutes the substance and scope of any practical spiritual or "religious" applications from within the paradigm of "*Mardukite Zuism*" specifically. In brief: all of the facets and developments and angles of approach provided by Joshua Free are interrelated.

Since notebooks for "*The Power of ZU*" were compiled and developed many years prior to "*Tablets of Destiny*" and "*Crystal Clear*" (and other recent summations), it will be immediately noticed by experienced *Seekers* (and/or returning readers) that the scope of "ZU" is actually treated in this volume as a reflection of one of its alternate definitions: "Spiritual-Life-Energy." In one sense, this is a supplemental use of the concept of "ZU" on ancient cuneiform tablets, when one combines the semantics for "ZU" (*knowing*) and "TU" (*Life*) to arrive at the "ZI" (and "TI") signs defining the "Life-breath" or "Vital Energy" of a being—the cuneiform sign literally describing the "chirping activity" of birds. As such, the current volume treats "ZU" as not only an "intellectual Awareness," but very broadly a state and condition of "Spiritual-Life-Energy" that we are maintaining in this Life-Existence-Experience as a whole.

From this context of "*Spiritual-Life-Energy,*" a person might choose to crossover to consider where else such a concept exists throughout the accessible mystical libraries and spiritual knowledge stores, such as *ki* or *chi* or *prana* or *Starfyre* &tc.—but it is clearly not the present intentions of Joshua Free to simply invite into our Systemology any and every application of "Spiritual-Life-Energy" encountered in history or esoteric lore. Such matters were actually already treated long ago from the author's own wide-angle view in the original *Grade I* materials—such as his notorious underground masterpiece: "*The Great Magical Arcanum.*"

At that initial grade of material, any practical or relevant knowledge base was explored for the fact that it existed and how it existed in relation to other paradigms; but it was not explored as a testament to any *one* preexisting paradigm as being the most direct or effective route toward some end, of which our most appropriate common universal "end" was determined to surround an idea of "*Ascension*."

> Whatever is found at the heart of Babylonian or Egyptian or Hermetic (or otherwise) interpretations of the Ancient Mystery School—the truest and highest ideals and "ends" are always in the direction of "*Ascension*"—in whatever manner that may be realized and relayed given the semantics, language and/or culture they are applied to.

Certainly, too, Joshua Free has expressed in numerous sources that this "Ascension" of "*Actualized Awareness*" is clearly not an "inevitability" outside of Self-directed efforts; that we *are* as Self-directed and Aware as we *are*, and that this is the only inevitability in our ability to consciously direct Self as, what is called, the "*Alpha Spirit*" during and after this current physical incarnation. It is in this same acute direction of an Actualized Ascension that we are headed to in NexGen Systemology—as a part of the spiritual technologies required to ensure a true spiritual evolution of the Human Condition.

The "*Pathway to Self-Honesty*" is what has uniquely defined the 21st Century paradigm of *Mardukite Zuism* and *Mardukite Systemology*—demonstrating its superiority as the preferred method of driving us forward into the future. Although it is *our* destiny to reach a superior state of *Self-Actualization*—to "walk among the gods"—the route or pathway that is our "*fate*" is ours alone to determine. Whatever detours and distractions we experience are entirely ours to decide—and the power and responsibility of such only thickens as we tread further and further on the *Pathway to Self-Honesty*.

Articles compiled for "_The Power of ZU_" may seem rudimentary when compared to the other texts found in this cycle of
materials—and yet the very fact that they are rudimentary
and set out as significant by the author suggests that these
points of fact are too often overlooked; or when they are
communicated, the importance or application to the greater
holistic whole is not properly relayed.

> In short: it has been found too often that the prelim-
> inary fundamentals of a methodology, and even the
> very basic principles and semantics applied to our
> Systemology are not _realized_ by an individual to the
> extent that is necessary to carry an increasing devel-
> opmental understanding and effective application of
> the "higher" lessons.

In the past—during the time of the Ancient Mystery School
—the issue of incremental learning and actualized experience was fully resolved with direct apprenticeships and
supervision; but, in a world of home-study courses and
readily obtainable books, it is often difficult to objectively
gauge a person's practical understanding—especially if little
feedback is directed back to the Office. It is sometimes difficult to prepare the right materials to fit the specific needs
of individuals across the board—yet, it seems that Joshua
Free has accomplished _just that_ in at least this volume. As
such, "_The Power of ZU_" is pointedly prepared as a matter of
clarification for those pursuing _Mardukite Zuism_ and _Mar-
dukite Systemology_ independent of direct involvement,
mentorship or _Systemology Piloting_.

> May this volume provide you with greater insights
> and certainty as you take up your own personal jour-
> ney on the _Pathway_!

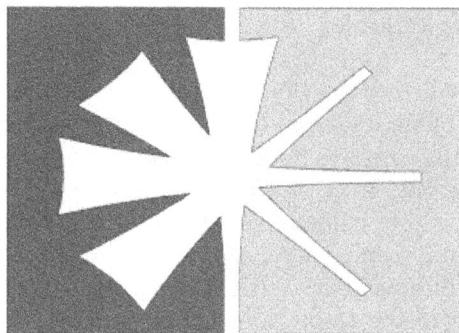

THE POWER OF

ZU

LECTURE SERIES

"The **premise** and pursuit of a <u>vital force</u> behind all of *Life*, the *Universe* and *Everything*, has fueled my own efforts toward a unique futurist *NexGen Systemology* since the days of my youth in the late 1990's. In spite of any other interests I may have applied to this quest along the way—ranging from **esoteric** occult mysticism to quantum **physics** and metapsychology—my personal aim has remained to codify the underlying *Systemology* of "**existence**." This, for me, represents a **holistic** and unified understanding of the *Universe* and **apparent** "**Reality**" as experienced from the "**Human Condition**"—and all those using the Human Condition to experience a Reality in *this* Physical Universe."

—Joshua Free

LECTURE ONE / INTRODUCTION
. :: **IN PURSIUT OF ZU** :: .
THE VITAL FORCE OF EXISTENCE

My interests to develop an improved *Systemology* for the Human Condition began during my teen years—during the 1990's. Although it would take at least another decade to officially codify anything of this direction directly, the underlying premise remained unchanged—and remains so today, even after all of the later developments have ensued.

It is a fact: that at the original **inception** of my research, I maintained my own personal purposes and reasons for uncovering and developing a modern *Mardukite* **paradigm** and applied *Systemology* for *myself*; and the sheer fact that the abundance of my underground work (even from its earliest years and versions) proved exceptionally useful and effective for others, is not hindered by the first fact.

In the mid-1990's, the apex of a "New Age" pop-culture surge was taking place—leading the way for me to assume a position early on in the underground scene as "Merlyn Stone." But, my interests did not solely occupy one track of **validating** "mysticism" or avenues of "magic" ("magick")—which I saw merely as one of many paradigms seeking to approach a higher **understanding** of *Life* and the *Physical Universe*—but it was unique on one point: it qualified the existence of something "more" or "beyond" or "higher than" ready available "beta-experience" and observable objective phenomenon restricted to matter in the Physical Universe—that which lies in the sensory range (perspective) of the Human Condition. Yet, as the public school system attempted to indoctrinate me deeper toward some specific academic goal, it became abundantly clear that a selection of any *one* of these available *paradigms* would force me further into an exclusionary **viewpoint** of observing *Life* and the *Universe* as some "effect" or another—but never getting any closer to a "cause." I was after the "*cause.*"

Although **physics**, quantum physics and higher scientific applications—such as "string theory"—were growing intellectual hobbies of mine, I found myself unable to get beyond my own disinterest in the intensive "mathematics" required to treat these subjects at an academic **level**. In fact, I found this to be the case for myself with most of the "physical sciences," because in my own mind, I did not believe that my own path, and the abilities it could unfold, should require such an intensive pursuit of chemical-calculus, or complex equations for unrealistic laboratory **conditions**, to be effective.

The **Ancient Mystery School** operated on principles or "**postulates**," which were only later qualified with **Babylonian**, Egyptian and Greek (*&tc.*) schools of mathematical philosophy—but these fundamentals of existence, and the original **knowledge** of the same, were not born from the equations; only validated by them.

I concluded that any important theorems or *a-priori axioms* would stand as themselves if they were true—and any supplemental demonstrations or "equation proofs" would only be necessary for certain **communications** of application or instruction. Even without these to support **objectively**: the facts behind them would be facts if they were indeed facts. Thus, I figured that a conceptual understanding at best—at least for my own purposes—was all that would be necessary regarding each of these fields. And while over the course of time, I would perhaps be called forth as no greater expert in any one of these fields than "the next guy," I have usually been able to apply this wide-angle view of understanding directly to my holistic work—and have found that it is, more often than not, recognized by readers that are more likely to receive this information in terms along such general lines of communication that they are already somewhat familiar with.

My strongest academic interests fell in the domain of what they considered "social sciences," but naturally I was interested in collecting all of the information I could about the "systems." I started earning college credit for attending courses at the nearby campus while I was still in high school. The only sure fit I could find at the beginning of this to satisfy requirements was a major in "psychology" with a minor in "philosophy." I also took all of the "anthropology" courses I could, figuring certainly that the "study of primitive man" should yield something of value to me—but aside from a potential career in "forensics" (if I were to better apply myself to memorizing all the human bones and such), I did not find any of my answers there. Not to mention: this was just at the turn of the century and millennium—and while I as attending one of my first "anthropology" courses, the entire class met up for extra credit to conduct an after-hours closed session preview of a "groundbreaking new" exhibit that was visiting our Denver museum, concerning the "latest and greatest" discovery in bridging the evolutionary gap in human history: "Lucy."

After high school and my run-ins and mentorships with most of the mystical-magical organizations in operation (accounts which have been recorded in my older literary installments), I spent the first few years of the new millennium **immersed** in traditional academics—all the while *Seeking* the specific **facets** I would require to compile my own working universal philosophy, which would hopefully result in an effectively applied one. My inspiration to attend such classes was driven by my ideas to shape the future of "creative psychology" (what I was calling "*metapsychology*"), strongly based on my researches into such as Carl Jung and Timothy Leary, to name a few; those that seemed to perhaps have gleaned something "true" about this thing called "consciousness"—the "Mind."

It seemed logical to me that an intellectual pursuit into the "Mind" would necessarily resolve what I needed to uncover about the "Human Condition"—and hopefully too, information that might unfold the **potentials** of the "Spirit." I was also reminded by several of those in my vicinity that if I did not acquire the "credentials" by academic superiors of our society, than I would be unable to make my desired contributions—or receive any financial contributions from others toward the development of this work. So, I cautiously agreed. But, when I got to college and embarked on this mission to earn an academic degree, I was... disappointed... nay, completely disillusioned regarding everything I thought I would be permitted to learn and encouraged to do.

After a few years of being taught by "behaviorist" professors and seeing all around me the evidence that any academic pursuits toward the "Mind" had been replaced solely by the "brain," I dropped the field altogether to complete a degree in a more mechanical education[*] that might pay a few bills while I pursued the research independently and in secret for many years even before emerging on the public scene with the "*Mardukite*" movement in 2008.

There are gaps of many accounted years before and after this pivotal inception of the modern "*Mardukite*" paradigm —and to this, my own answer is that **attention** has been consistently been put into the development of true and faithful, complete and effective, relevant and futurist applied spiritual technology behind "**Mardukite Zuism**," called "*Systemology*"—or else "*Mardukite Systemology*."

I then set out to develop my own *Systemology*—except it was not "my own"; it was the "Universe." But my academic background did not catch up with the spiritual (or metaphysical) Truth that I knew something of from direct experience—and yet I was at a great loss for finding the right words and **semantics** to communicate anything of it directly. Whenever I turned toward established sciences and philosophies and preexisting *-isms*, I would reach a "barrier." Each set of semantics belonged to one or another paradigm; each operated in an exclusion to all others.

---

[*] "*HVAC Technologies, Associate of Applied Sciences.*"

Although there were certain concepts, principles and axioms that I might "cherry-pick" along the journey—certain facets that I might find a use for within my own developments—there was no way of accomplishing what I set out to do by "fixing" or "extending" some preexisting semantic paradigm, philosophy or science. Trying to attempt to do so from within any one of these paradigms was most certainly folly—because I had already read the works and observed efforts of many others who had already gone forth on that same premise into whatever specific avenue they pursued. None were directly successfully in doing anything other than extending or advancing one particular paradigm or another—only effective in furthering the **fragmentation** and applying deeper intellectual exclusion. Such would have been directly **counter-productive** to my own **intention**.

There were too many flaws with the conventional **methodology** inherent in conventional education and it became clear that there was also no room for innovation, progression or advancement within the **institutions** that instructed in **patterned** "copy-and-paste" from previous generations; the same previous generations that sent us speeding down to plummet into a pool of unnecessary suffering, destruction and devastation. I wasn't interested in being *like* Freud. I didn't want to starve dogs into drooling to the sound of bells. I found no logic in torturing the animal kingdom as a means to any worthwhile **realizations** for the Human "*psyche*," which was a word originally attached to the "*soul*" or "*spirit*"—or at the very least the "Mind"— of the Human Condition, but of which could not be found outright in any single accepted academic science or applied philosophy. These were the type of people that spent millions of dollars to prove that hungry rats will chase through mazes to find cheese. Every attempt to demonstrate something of value with human subjects—such as the "guards versus prisoner experiment"—proved to be a disaster. Certainly, this allegedly "higher education" would offer no actual avenues "out" of this programmed state of low *Awareness* that humanity had **succumb** to.

Had I thought that switching my major and minor would have been an improvement, I would have—but the ceaseless conjecture of existing classical philosophy was of only small benefit directly. Of these, the one that stood apart was *Logic* —and perhaps the premise behind the schools of **epistemology**, but they did not exclusively provide answers; simply methods of which answers might be better **evaluated** objectively. Most of the other relevant schools of philosophy remained in the domain of "philosophy" and not "science" simply because they remained outside the realm of empirical or **external** observation. As a result, the schools (or paradigms) were each far reaching in their own directions and only furthered an idea of the perpetual "maybe" by existing on opposing ends of some dualistic polar **dichotomy**.

This idea of "dualism" was rampant in every field; each piece of data treated in exclusion to another within a **parameter** or fixed-range along some line—usually between perceived extremes. They did not provide answers with "yes" or "no" and instead kept human understanding—and its state of **Actualized** *Awareness*—suspended in a state of "maybe" in perpetuity. I was after something else; something which I did not even discover a word for until after I left the realm of academia: I was after a knowledge of everything as could be plotted on a "*monistic continuum*" of a singular unified force.

Results of this pursuit were actually discovered to be only the beginning, but a monumental milestone nonetheless: an effective **"Standard Model"** for *Systemology*. Early versions of this knowledge were originally presented (while research emphasis was still actively involved in the "*Mardukite Grade II*" phase of 2009) as the "*Reality Engineering*" series of lectures. Quite relevantly, this same series of lectures— portions of which appeared in introductory sections of our "*Complete Anunnaki Bible,*" other portions contributing to the later materials of "*Systemology: The Original Thesis*" and then finally a companion textbook by the same name (released to the underground in 2013)—later prompted the actual "New

Thought" division of the *"Mardukite Chamberlains"* (*Mardukite Research Organization* governed by *Mardukite Ministries*) that developed as the *"NexGen Systemology Society."*

When we compare the slow, but exponential, developmental **timeline** marking improved codification of *NexGen Systemology* since my original conception of the idea, what has really changed between "then" and "now"—as evident between older materials, such as *"Systemology: The Original Thesis"* and *"Liber-R"** versus the newer progressive innovations like *"**Tablets of Destiny**"* and *"**Crystal Clear**"*—is essentially a unification of the "Standard Model" with a discovery of something previously overlooked, but buried directly within the "Divine Wisdom" alluded to in our ancient **Mesopotamian** *Grade II* work: and it is called "ZU." When this could be coherently presented as a foundation for *Grade III Mardukite Systemology*, a relay of the discoveries were immediately released as *"Tablets of Destiny"* and its companion course textbook, *"Crystal Clear"*—but it took many years of quiet covert behind-the-scenes refinement to actually reach these "newer" developments.

Within this brief series of articles, I intend to provide some of the previous untold background and additional applications of research that were present in rudimentary experiments for *"Mardukite Systemology,"* long before our more recent and continuing developments in *"Systemology Processing."* In the past we were unable to successfully unite a "Standard Model" with a **singularity** because the research methods kept us away from anything that might denote *polarity*. But this has been since rectified by our understanding of activity present in the Physical Universe in connection to one specific aspect of interconnectivity that is somehow extended from a Spiritual Universe.

We recognize now that the polarity is necessary to apparent action and is not the same as the **"fragmentation"** that is

---

* Recently reissued as *"Novem Portis: Necronomicon Revelations"* 10th Anniversary Collector's Hardcover by Joshua Free.

present in our knowledge and understanding. That we can now (in *Grade III*) demonstrate what we call the "**ZU-line**" across the "Standard Model" is a significance that can never be overstated; for it is what is allowing for all progressive future development of this philosophy as a applied spiritual technology—essentially the only "NexGen" paradigm that is not only taking into account all that is already swiftly considered (above in this report) but also the future **fate** of the Human Condition in arriving at its destination at a higher state of *Awareness* and ultimately a spiritual evolution.

There are so many **paramount** matters affecting humanity today—and one could surely ceaselessly string a dissertation regarding little else—but the truth is that all of these "problems" inherent in the Human Condition and directly regarding its physical environment on planet Earth (and throughout the **Cosmos** and beyond) can actually be resolved if we take the steps toward an elevation in our capacity for *Actualized Awareness*. Assuming this can not expeditiously be conducted on each of the billions of **individuals** sharing an experience of the Human Condition around the planet—there are other steps that must be taken by those hearing the call and **willing** to assume the **responsibility** toward co-creating the future course of our existence. All of this is a group effort based on the singular intentions of its members united together. This requires true communication of ideas, energy and power across a worldwide network to be effective—but it very clearly and most certainly begins with a strong and healthy individual; which is also something that will be emphasized within this specific series of reports.

The strength and continuation of the human and hybrid-human species; the strength of the society and community it occupies; the strength of our organizations representing and carrying *Mardukite Zuism* and *Mardukite Systemology* into the future; all of these are dependent on the strength and integrity of the individuals—as always, it begins and ends with *Self*.

The ancients instructed their initiates to:
Know Thyself; Through Self, Know All.

I can think of no greater, loftier, more applicable ideal to achieve these ends, than this journey we are now on—*The Pathway to Self-Honesty*...and *beyond!*

LECTURE TWO

. :: **THE NATURE OF ZU** :: .

IDENTIFYING THE RADIANT ENERGY

Logic and *math* that surrounds the "Standard Model" used in *Mardukite Zuism* and *Mardukite Systemology* is validated by the application of a "theoretical construct" we call the "*ZU-line*." This "line" is described as such only to demonstrate its **continuity** and interconnectivity as an "**Identity**" and is not necessarily any kind of a actual or ethereal "cord" &tc.

It very well may be, on some **level** of energetic observation, but any "vision" of such, when using "astral vision" for example, is entirely the "construct" or "**thought-form**" of the observer. If there is some type of "cord" connecting the "I" of the **Alpha Spirit** to some physical body ("**genetic vehicle**"), it could only be of *one type* of substance. We may conclude this as a result of *Self-Honest* examination of all that we can observe directly concerning **Cosmic Law** in the Physical Universe—and as a result of what we are able to calculate for using applied spiritual technologies alluded to on the "*Tablets of Destiny*," which surpass former philosophies of "metaphysics," &tc. This all leads us to a point of understanding that there is only one actual force or essence connecting the "Spiritual" and the "Physical" along a **continuum**: and that is "*ZU*."

We derive our philosophic and semantic understanding of "ZU" directly from ancient Mardukite Wisdom Tablets found buried beneath Babylonian **cuneiform** literature (studied in the *Grade II* materials of the "*Mardukite Core*"). In fact, many of these ancient spiritual **allegories** may be found within the context of ancient Babylonian "Anunnaki" mythology—and hence the emergence of modern "*Mardukite Zuism*" to satisfy what is otherwise found to be a socio-spiritual gap: since for all of the books and discussions and pop-culture television shows reaching millions with some idea of an "alien **religion**" or "Anunnaki Spiritual Tradition," we do not actually find many valid avenues for a *Seeker* to explore such as a true and present "Reality."

Likewise, it should be understood that the more advanced processes and continuing developments of "*Mardukite Systemology*" that are applied as "spiritual techniques" directly to the religious/spiritual connotations of "*Mardukite Zuism*" are not dependent on personal adherence or **participation** with any revivalist "religion" in order to be valid as an effective spiritual science in its own right; just as the concepts and validity behind exercises of "prayer" and "meditation" are not specific to any one paradigm or tradition, even if each one provides their own flavor or theme of instruction toward such methods.

There are many mystics, magicians, priests, priestesses, shamans and esoteric intellectuals that have come upon some **degree** of understanding regarding Cosmic Law in the past—and those who have seen something of its significance in regards to *Life* and *Actualized Awareness* have gone in search for the "Spiritual Life Energy" that is not accounted for in the descriptions and axioms that describe the Physical Universe. The biochemical and cellular matters are accounted for regarding the organism; there are even ways of understanding the **motors** and nervous system, but again, only concerning the "genetic vehicle" itself—and nothing concerning the "Spiritual Life Energy" or "Vital Energy" that is not physical; for, in science, we have no true physical understanding of "**consciousness**" or "*Actualized Awareness*" directly, and anything that may be determined in regards to "Self" may just as easily be distorted by fragmented sensory experience and memory. This led us to seek effective methods of "**defragmentation**," because without which we would not actually have any certainty about our "rising above" or beyond what it means to be a reactive-response programmed and **conditioned** Identity trapped within the **beta-*Awareness*** of a physical body.

60

In the past, many other metaphysical, esoteric and occult attempts have been made in developing a working philosophy or applied spiritual technology to varying degrees of success. It is easy to find traces of this in any literature that relates to some "Vital Energy" or "Spiritual Life Energy" under the context of: aether, aethyrs, astral light, azoth, clear light, divine energy, divine light, divine spark, god-force, glama, god-mind, kia, lifeforce, logos, orgone, prana, ruach, spirit, starfire, subtle energy, universal energy and vril. All of these word-names have been used in the past to describe a unique "Spiritual Life Energy" that connects the "Other" or "Spiritual Universe" (the *alpha* or *metaphysical*) to the "Physical Universe" (or *beta-existence*) that we readily experience from the perspective of the physical body, which is composed of physical matter of the physical universe and biochemically processes physical energy in the physical universe.

The name that we have chosen to demonstrate this "Vital Energy" or "Spiritual Life Energy" is based on the oldest written language from the inception of the social and cultural systems defining the "Human Condition" in ancient Mesopotamia. The name we have chosen is very specifically "ZU" and it may be used in place of any of the others—when following the knowledge of the "Standard Model"—as a semantic for understanding exactly what we are in search of in order to fully understand, appreciate and apply the wisdom of the Anunnaki "*Tablets of Destiny.*"

Δ Δ Δ Δ Δ Δ

Whenever "Spiritual Life Energy" or "Vital Lifeforce" is encountered within the scope of "*Mardukite Zuism*" and "*Mardukite Systemology,*" it is treated as "*ZU.*" This ancient **Sumerian** cuneiform expression is used to denote the unique "*Life Awareness*" that connects Spiritual Existence to Physical Existence. These two "existences" are appropriately defined on the *Arcane Tablets* as "AN" for the "Spiritual Universe" and "KI" for the "*Physical Universe*"—although some scholars in the past have restricted their understanding of these terms as literally "heaven" and "earth" respectively. The advanced interpretations provided by the "Standard Model" in its relationship to the ALL and the LAW as described in the body of the ancient Babylonian "Epic of Creation," has also led us to equate the two "existences" in terms of "Alpha" and "Beta"—as explained in more detail in former texts, such as *"Tablets of Destiny"* and *"Crystal Clear."*

The word "ZU" is sometimes applied in difference contexts, although each of them is still true to the original meaning behind the word. In one sense, we have the application of a broad stream, **band** or ray of "Spiritual Life Energy" that is considered the "Vital Lifeforce" of a living organism. It is also a reference to the verb "to know" as in the "ability and capacity to know" or the extent to which someone is "filled with knowledge."

For our modern purposes of "codifying" the *Systemology* at hand into a coherent and applicable methodology, this idea has been most strongly expressed with the word "Awareness"—specifically what we refer to as *Actualized Awareness*. When we use the *"ZU-line"* as a description of *Awareness*, particularly the *Awareness* as it is applied to beta-existence (or the Physical Universe), a person's capacity or effective ability to direct personal ZU is also considered a reflection of their "personal magnetism"—which is understood to be a *radiation* of this "Vital Lifeforce" into one's environment in the Physical Universe and interactions with other *Life*.

Although the religious applications of *"Mardukite Zuism"* and the applied spiritual technologies of *"Mardukite Systemology"* (and the full scope of *"NexGen Systemology"*) are intended to provide an effective workable philosophy of *Life*, the *Universe* and *Everything*—it will be immediately noticed by those so inclined that the methods and **realizations** presented throughout the esoteric library of *Systemology* does actually provide many applications and validations—and perhaps even more *answers*—regarding traditional "occult sciences," "mysticism," "energy healing" and "New Age metaphysics" than these paradigms offer from within themselves. Although we do not necessarily treat the "ritualism" and "cultural **symbols**" of traditional "magic" in *Systemology*, it is interesting that taking up this wide-angle perspective—that includes "ZU" and the "Standard Model"—necessarily describes or accounts for various phenomenon that could very well explain a significant amount of what people might consider "supernatural" or "Otherworldly" (if they do not have this higher level of understanding and *Awareness*).

It is not our intention to directly validate, **invalidate** or otherwise explain specifics of any of this phenomenon as it has been described by the semantics of other paradigms, other than an effort to strongly express the fact that the further a *Seeker* travels on the *Pathway to Self-Honesty*, the greater of an understanding is attained, including realizations concerning many of these other facets of existence, which just seem to "line up" in our **reasoning** thereafter. They do not require as much attention at these higher "Grades" of work because they are no longer treated as a "Mystery."

The essays revised for this volume are meant to inspire or cultivate a greater understanding and appreciation for what we are calling "ZU" within this *NexGen* semantic paradigm. By introducing the ancient wisdom and universal truths under this context—as a fresh concept or terminology—it is far easier to repair **erroneous** and faulty programmed understanding of the same *Universes* without having to spend unnecessary energy in reshaping thousands of years of cultural vocabulary and the manner of its reception and understanding by the **individual**.

Ours is a preferable approach, even in light of the fact that some individuals will find it mentally taxing to tackle this field or study under the guise of these "obscure" ancient terms. I can assure the *Seeker* (and reader) that it is no less

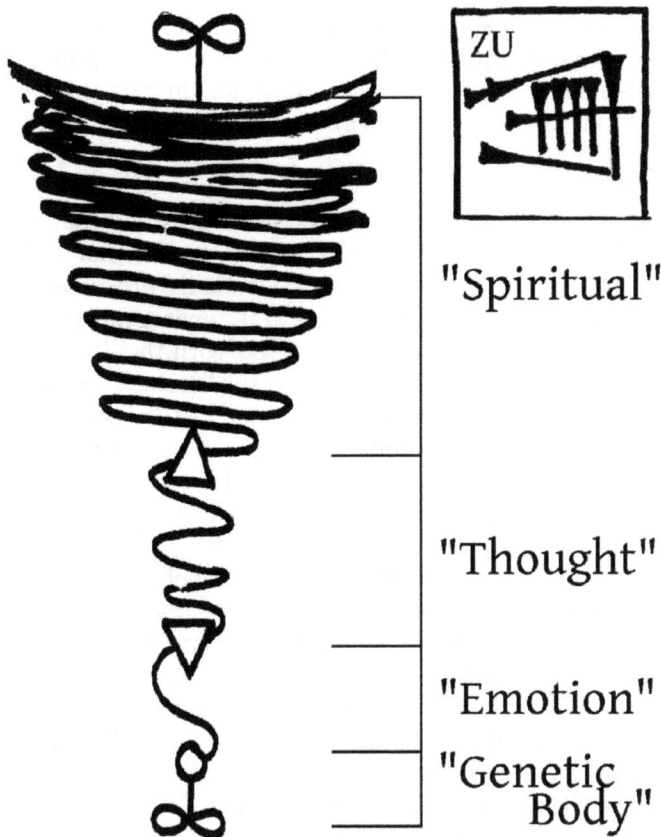

"Spiritual"

"Thought"

"Emotion"

"Genetic Body"

complicated or less ambiguous to apply any of the other terms previously used in related esoteric lore, such as "ruach" or "orgone" or "vril" and so forth—each of which would also require an extensive background lesson in cultural language and mythographic understanding to even be close to carrying the same effectiveness for *Systemology*.

In one sense, we refer to ZU as the primary "Spiritual Life Energy" that is present in our known existence, but which necessarily has a source or cause that is **exterior** to what is considered the "Physical Universe." We consider this ZU to be a permeating principle of *Awareness* that is beyond the physical energy and physical matter that we **associate** with physical **manifestation**. Clearly there is an element of "consciousness" that is not accounted for in the elements, chemicals and substance forms that are **identified** as "physical."

However, in saying this, it should be understood that ZU is not literally and exclusively the "Mind" itself, either—which is a "system" of manifestation that actually processes, carries or otherwise "communicates" ZU apparent as personal "*Awareness.*" It is easy to associate ZU with the "Mind" because—as we may demonstrate with the "Standard Model"—it is actually the point where the "***Master Control Center***" (MCC) of the "Mind-System" is plotted at "4.0" on our "*ZU-line*," which directly corresponds to the **threshold** point between "physical" and "spiritual" existences.

In addition to representing the element behind what some individuals of the mystical persuasion have considered "cosmic consciousness" or other broad **existential** definitions, ZU also represents an individual "*Lifeforce*" or specific "Spiritual Life Energy" that imbues, impinges or otherwise **controls** the physical manifestations of "*Life.*" It is a combination of the specific, subjective and personal terms, along with those existential, universal and cosmic ones that has given rise to a plethora of cultural mythologies and mystical traditions in the past concerning unique beliefs about the phenomenon and **presence** of this energy in the observable universe.

In early lectures and materials for "*NexGen Systemology,*" this activity was referred to as "**perturbation**" because we are only able to observe and sense manifestations and behaviors of phenomenon that are otherwise being influenced, directed or controlled from an *exterior*—or essentially "unseen" and "undetectable"—source.

This "Other" is what many refer to when speaking of the "spiritual" and "metaphysical" or even the "supernatural"—

although it should be noted that no phenomenon in the Physical Universe is truly "super-natural." The *naturalness* may simply operate by some unrecognized aspect of Cosmic Law. Cosmic Law automation specifically governs all expressions of manifestation in the Physical Universe, regardless of the source or directed control of that energy from an *exterior* source.

Δ Δ Δ Δ Δ Δ Δ

There are some perceptive individuals across the timeline of Human history that have, in some way, caught a "sense" that there is an additional element behind all that we are able to observe in the Physical Universe. Even those "higher minds" that first conceived of the sciences and philosophies —that are now stretched out thinly in their own directions by their followers—were able to recognize this "cosmic code" or "universal agent" that imbued certain aspects or concentrations of physical energy and matter with something that has only been religiously treated as "spirit" or the "Cosmic Mind," but of which we are now able to better identify as ZU in our wider more **encompassing** holistic systems-theory approach. This is not to slight out all of what has formerly been presented by the innovators and creators and "*Actualized*" individuals—which were mainly restricted to a combined semantic "understanding-as-language" barrier for themselves and their own time periods in effectively *communicating* what they *knew* on an objective **static** written medium. In spite of what experiences, levels of *Awareness* or other realizations that may be achieved by an individual, their own understanding—and their ability to share such "reality" with other individuals—will always come back to the communication of information and energy, both "**internally**" among one's own personal systems and in any interactions with other systems.

However, we should not slight out any truly *Self-Honest* attempts made by our predecessors of lore, especially when they have caught a "sense" of this "Other," regardless of how they chose to classify or incorporate this understanding into their work. Even when it could not be incorporated directly, such as the **consideration** of "spiritual values" in "physical equations," we are at least certain that these individuals held such points of fact in mind while **participating** in the "Realm" appropriately. We see many aspects of the *epistemology* held by Rene Descrates to simply include "God" as the word accounting for all *Infinity* in the *Other*, particularly as he was writing for a predominantly Christian audience. We notice similar methods taken by the Scottish Episcopalian Minister, Reverend Robert Kirk, in his account of the Elven-Faerie "commonwealth." Considerable attention is given in his literature toward persuading the reader to separate their idea of elves and fairies from the "demons" of biblical mythology, an upgrade from former beliefs that the Church sought to maintain. Of course, the control of intellectual **authority** strongly shifted to scientists and medical professionals during the Industrial Age, but many of these figures were also quite aware of something in the back of all their calculations; something that could not be present in their physical calculations.

Consider the German-born theoretical physicist and philosopher, Max Planck (1858-1947), who was awarded the Nobel Prize (in 1918) for the inception of "*quantum theory*," which soon after became the baseline and standard for researches into atomic and sub-atomic particles. We would expect a very mechanistic description of a "**clockwork** universe"—just as we were prone to see in the past. But, that is not what provided the innovations to better understand functions of the Physical Universe. Plank writes:

> "All matter originates and exists by virtue of a force which brings the particles of atoms to **vibration**— holding this minute atomic solar system together. We must assume behind this force the existence of a consciousness and intelligent 'mind'. This 'mind' is the 'Matrix' of all matter."

Critical observations were made by the more philosophic-minded of the science community. But many of these original concepts—some that are now often revived under new semantics—were threshed out of the original "approved" methodologies due to their esoteric qualities. And once we started separating "pseudo-sciences" from the "academics" we started to see a larger gap take place concerning intellectual developments—many of which today are simply speeding up or improving upon existing models, and those taken from covertly recovered technologies, but of which are not the result of, or providing further methods of, true human innovation toward an actualized evolution that is not dependent on external technologies for it to ensue. Such "external" modes of mechanistic thinking are certainly going to only entrap the "Human Spirit" further into clockwork barriers that cannot be recovered from so long as their automation remains outside control.

The "Human Condition" was plunged deeper into a mechanistic worldview as a counter-effort to the "mysticism" and "esoteric occultism" rising up during the Renaissance—which was in itself a counter-effort against social suppression by the Church. These cycles continue endlessly when left to their own accord—and that is how the systems work, given their movement and action by following a basic pendulum swing. But this activity and motion should not be treated as "mysterious," because if we are meant to solidify any type of understanding about our *Self* and *Life* and the *Universe*, it should be understood that there is a pattern and ordering beneath everything that exists, and when it relates to the Physical Universe, we refer very specifically to this code, pattern and/or governance of the 'Matrix' as "*Cosmic Law.*"

The means and manner by which this "Cosmic Law" is communicated throughout the Universe is what seems to have the scientific community confounded—or at least at a glass ceiling—since they are in the habit of observing, measuring and playing with accessible effects that they "can see" rather than encroach on the realm of "philosophy" in any way. Given how many of the mathematical, logical and physical sciences have been literally pulled out of their resting places among the philosophical schools, there is very little that remains in the domain of "philosophy" today, aside from the "immaterial" and "metaphysical." The actual "I" that was discovered in the folds of classical philosophy has never left its nestled zone there; the scientists have never, not once, been able to get the "I" under the microscope.

There is a "consciousness" present—which we refer very specifically as "*Awareness*" in the Mardukite paradigms—and it very closely relates to what we are treating as ZU. We speak quite loosely now of substance-forms, matter, energy and metaphysical forces—but this understanding has not always been so casual and common. In fact it was all once very esoteric and only understood in the semantic terms of "magic" and "mysticism." That is not to say there is no validity to the methods they represent; but the position of the Observer (in such paradigms) is still looking at effects as "mysterious" and from some "unknown cause."

Even if a cause is attributed to some other element or particle or spirit, it is assumed that the "magician" themselves is not being placed in the position of "cause," and many of the grimoires warn about essentially becoming a victim to one's own "effect" in the process. It is surprising that many of the methods are effective to any extent when they are operated from such low-energy points of "fear" or even "anger," which seem to be the primary emotional motivators behind these "lower" forms of "magic."

The "*Pathway to Self-Honesty*" that is described in the modern tradition of "*Mardukite Zuism*" and the spiritual technology of "*Mardukite Systemology*" focuses on "personal defragmentation" and by doing so, increasing the certainty of the individual to control their *Self-direction*. In the past, we have been taught that certain forms of physical energy and matter will combine to form *Life* and *Awareness*, but it has been demonstrated in *Systemology* that this necessarily comes from a "higher" point of cause as source, and a point of spiritual control that is *exterior* to what we are able to calculate concerning the Physical Universe.

It is demonstrated that a continuum of ZU
—a singular expression of a specific type of energy—
is directed across all existences or Universes.

At certain levels of heavy solid concentration nearest the "continuity levels" of the **entropic** Physical Universe, we have very solid manifestations of this energy, and at higher frequencies we see that the power of ZU interacts less and less directly onto the lower "matter" itself, but it *radiates*—that is to say that it sets off a "chain reaction" along the ZU-line that reaches other frequency types. In brief:

ZU excites ZU at other levels of frequency via a
chain-reaction. This is what makes the
interconnected activity function as all of the
interrelated systems of existence—any existence.

It is this concept—of treating ZU as a *radiation*, much like the "electromagnetic **spectrum**"—that allowed effective developments in *Systemology* to unfold as an understanding of the "ZU-line."

This realization is what turned our older "Standard Model" into something workable and applicable for our purposes as opposed to remaining simply an aesthetically pleasing *kabbalistic* model to post up on our refrigerators as an "A+" artistic accomplishment.

Such vanity would hardly serve any purposes here in promoting some beneficial "gains" for those that are actively seeking ways to improve their own development toward "Self-**Actualization**" and assist with helping usher in the *new* "Crystal Age" of humanity that is critically needed if we are to continue our spiritual evolution toward a direction of reunification with our spiritual source and the *Self-Honest* actualized realization of operating the *Self* in a crystal clear state of *Self* from and as *Self*—and perhaps for the first time in our extensive spiritual journey, which has spanned many lives and universes.

It is perhaps in *this* lifetime that we will finally *realize* and *actualize* what we have been searching for all of this time; and what we will discover is sure to be the first thing—the first *real* thing—ever to carry with us beyond a physical **incarnation.**

LECTURE THREE

. :: **THE POWER OF ZU** :: .

LIFEFORCE OF THE PHYSICAL UNIVERSE

A concise summation of the precise "spiritual philosophy" present behind *Mardukite Systemology* as paradigm and tradition is expertly stated in <u>*Mardukite Zuism: Brief Introduction*</u>—based on the introductory "<u>*Tablets of Destiny*</u>" chapter-lesson (lecture) summaries:

> "The Spiritual Universe ('AN') of 'metaphysical' or 'spiritual' matter and 'metaphysical' or 'spiritual' energy and the Physical Universe ('KI') of 'physical' matter and 'physical' energies are existentially independent of each other, maintaining a single **channel**, conduit or connection, which is 'Alpha Spirit' *Awareness* as 'Spiritual Life Energy' or 'ZU'. The 'Alpha Spirit' engages a 'ZU-line', a spiritual lifeline of ZU energy to a 'genetic vehicle' or '**organic** body' to experience 'beta-existence'—the 'Physical Universe'."

In *Systemology*, we often tend to refer to the "physical body" as the "genetic vehicle" of an "*Alpha Spirit.*" As such, we say that certain physical organic life systems of this "genetic vehicle" are actually controlled by the Alpha Spirit using a continuous lifeline of ZU energy. It is further expressed from the above source that:

> "A 'spiritual continuum' or 'conduit channel' of ZU—absolute 'Spiritual Life Energy'—directly links our *Awareness* levels of 'I-AM', 'True Self' or 'Alpha Spirit' with the degrees of motion and variation in the Physical Universe. The 'Alpha Spirit'—or 'soul identity'—*is* the 'I' or 'Self' connected to the operation and control of the organic physical body or 'genetic vehicle'."

A "Systemology of Physics" is introduced within the *Grade III* materials—such as "*Tablets of Destiny*"—that mainly pertains to the interaction (or communication) of energy between two primary principles of manifestation: *substance* and *motion*. But these are the observed principles only; they do not directly account for the third and necessary principle of manifestation: *consciousness* or *Awareness*. It is only when we consider all three principle aspects of manifestation—*substance, motion* and *Awareness*—that we are able to effective use our "Standard Model" as an appropriate estimation of Reality. And it is only when we realize that there is a ZU-force present in each one of these aspects, that we see any singularity or unification taking place in this reasoning.

>—As a *substance*, ZU is the "Cosmic Code" and "intelligent design" that programs all "things" to have its "forms."

>—As a *motion*, ZU is the energetic activity, exchange of information and interactive "communications" that vibrate within and radiate from "forms" and carry them in "**space**."

>—As a *consciousness* (*Awareness*), ZU is the "vital life-force" and essential spiritual energy that allows a perspective of an "Observer" to exist, which will then **differentiate** "forms" and calculate their "motions."

In this present series of supplemental reports[*] (lectures), we are primarily focusing on the third aspect of ZU, which is the "*Spiritual Life Energy*" that we recognize as the unique "*Vital Lifeforce*" present in organic living forms—or else "*Lifeforms*." These organic "*Lifeforms*" are treated as "genetic vehicles" that are under the **command** of the "Self." Personal "fragmentation" can ensue when the "Self" (*Alpha Spirit*) is not demonstrating its own **Self-determined** control of the organic genetic vehicle it most closely **identifies** with; in fact, it may so intensely identify with the genetic organism that it loses its own *Self-directed (Actualized) Awareness* to the automation and functions inherent in the *Lifeform* for its own level of "beta-Awareness."

---

[*] Transcripts first released as Systemology Air-Command Tech Report.

We can establish that there is a design and program behind substances and motions easily enough, but what most individuals—at this stage of development—are primarily interested in, is the applications and functions of this "ZU chain-reaction" by **WILL**. The "Systemology of WILL" is introduced in "_Crystal Clear._" It is not the "I" or _Alpha Spirit_ directly, but it is the spiritual equivalent for _Self_ to the "effort" demonstrated by the other "beta" systems and motors —connected along the "_ZU-line_" or ZU continuum—as they manifest in the Physical Universe. As a result—and with the assistance of the "Standard Model"—we might better realize _how_ this singular universal energetic force actually exists along an entire spectrum of potential manifestation, very similar to the way we view the EM-electomagnetic spectrum in the physical science.

The difference, however, between the "Standard Model" and the paradigms provided by traditional sciences, is that our holistic _Systemology_ also accounts for the other aspects that do not fit the "maths" of beta-physics. Therefore, these physical sciences have not yet been able to completely unify an understanding of the singular "Force."

We do not consider our model, or the field of _Systemology_, as exclusive to some immaterial intellectual fanciful "metaphysics"; it most necessarily includes data for "spiritual" (or metaphysical) existence, but also very much applies to the Physical Universe. It is only as a result of the physical sciences choosing to separate their understanding (that exists in isolation as a tradition of _beta-knowledge_) that makes anything else "beyond" such known paradigms seem very mystical and mysterious. Yet, when many who have walked this _Pathway_ before have very successfully demonstrated that it is not any more supernatural than if we were to compare work and innovations of a more primitive civilization with the same Human Condition more recently on the timeline, concerning something demonstrated and experienced, such as "space travel." Certainly such vistas of reasoning would seem "supernatural" to the less educated population, or a civilization that maintained no tangible reality communicated on such subjects—and yet we very much know the technology today to be one of very real and imaginable possibility.

The only thing that has changed along our genetic timeline (considering the "Human Condition" as a "*species*") is the capacity and its contents of higher knowledge and personal "*Self-Actualization*" regarding a universe that has otherwise not changed a bit in terms of its own objective potential.

> Only the *Lifeform* that is demonstrating some
> application of *Awareness* is
> changing in their *willingness* for things "*to be.*"

If we were to chart the highest frequency potentials of personal ZU, they would be roughly equivalent to positions on the *Standard Model/ZU-line* marked as "control centers"—explained in detail within the primary *Grade III* textbooks: "*Tablets of Destiny*" and "*Crystal Clear*"—but there is an **optimum** peak that may be communicated at each level along the entire spectrum. This is essentially what happens naturally as a *Seeker* is taking steps toward greater degrees of *Self-defragmentation*. It happens in such a way now, as part of the progressive developments taken in this new field of *NexGen Systemology*, that a full "doctorate" level nuts-and-bolts understanding of the methodology is *not* actually necessary in order to obtain effective results from its procedures. However, since we cannot always expect that the conditions that it is applied to in everyday life will be specifically covered in such a general book, it is often a great benefit for an operator or technician of this Tech to learn as much as possible about the "ins-and-outs" of the work—which is, for example, one of the primary purposes behind the literary articles comprising this volume.

Δ Δ Δ Δ Δ Δ Δ

Since our intention is to provide a general introduction to

the subject and nature of ZU through this series of articles (lectures), it is equally important for us to clearly define what ZU is not. Because as soon as we have begun to present this *NexGen* methodology of applied spiritual technology, we immediately have a series of readers (*Seekers*) that are going to directly confuse the nature and function of ZU with something or another that they have picked up from the explanations and demonstrations provided in other traditions and paradigms. In fact, we are careful in our "Standard Model" to not confuse the actual nature of ZU—or the ZU-line—with any direct expressions or interactions with, for example, the *Alpha Spirit*, the WILL, the Mind-System, or the biochemical organism.

There is a circulatory communication of ZU present within and as each "level" or "aspect" of existence and manifestation, but not one of them *is* ZU. This communication of ZU is directly present in each "principle of manifestation"—*substance*, *motion* and *Awareness*—but it is not any *one* these either. We plot the positive spectrum of ZU—or *ZU-line*—on the "Standard Model" from *Zero* (a continuity of the Physical Universe) all the way to *Infinity*. Demonstrations of this expression and interaction are identifiable at any distinguishable point or degree on this continuum. It is only when a *Seeker* (or any individual) fixes their understanding of ZU to only one expression or observed activity that we reach such erroneous exclusive conclusions like, "ZU is electricity" or "ZU is the soul" or "ZU is the nerve energy in the body" and so forth. While it may have some relationship with any and all of these, we cannot treat its nature as being specifically intended for any one of these manifestations exclusively. Whatever can be known about ZU with certainty must apply "across the boards" (or more correctly, across the "ZU-line") as a constant, even if the interactions at each existential point, degree or level of interaction have their own peculiarities in relation to each **relative** state.

Aside from the direction and composition of the Alpha Spirit itself (near one end of the observed spectrum of our continuum, we mark as "7.0"), and aside from the physical delivery of ZU to nourish and maintain the genetic physical organism (near the other end of the spectrum at its most physical range between "1.0" and "0.1"), there is only *one* primary factor that relays a communication of ZU between the "Spirit" and the "Body" and that *is* the "Mind-System." Although we would be incorrect in, again, identifying ZU directly with the "Mind" itself, however: ZU energy is communicated or **transmitted** directly via "Thoughts"—and by "thoughts" we do not mean the "Mind System" as a whole, and certainly not the "brain." We may refer to processes and functions of these other organs and systems, but only that they promote, alter and/or affect the nature of ZU expressed in transmission. For some, it is easier to consider this level of ZU as the "stuff that thoughts are made of."

Some *Seekers* have best understood the nature of ZU in relation to *Awareness*—at least as it is applies to the individual and their own spiritual *Lifeforce*. This is probably the most accurate representation of the Force as it applies to a "Spiritual Life Energy" imposing upon, or intervening with, the range of existence that we consider the "Physical Universe." We know from our model that there is an absolute source of ZU in all existence—and it is the only "absolute" that we can actually be certain of in existence—which is called ABZU on the old cuneiform tablets. It roughly translates to "Abyss" by most mythographers and scholars in the academic community. When using esoteric semantics, it is referred to as the "Infinity of Nothingness"; and when we investigate further esoteric meaning behind the original cuneiform sign, we discover another secret definition: *Father of*—or *Heart of* —ZU. Essentially we are treating the "Infinity of Nothingness" (meaning infinite latent **potentiality**; so "nothing" in particular) as an "*Infinite Source*" of ZU.

If we consider what this means in the "Standard Model," there is an Infinite amount of ZU **extant** at ("8")—which is the point marked as the extent of conceivable existence, even the "metaphysical" or "Spiritual Universe."

At the point where we find a "peak" extend from this "*Infinity*" as an individuation, we mark the "I" or "I-AM" as the "*Alpha Spirit*" at ("7"). Although not an "*Infinite Source,*" the *Alpha Spirit* maintains a very significant capacity for ZU at its highest clearest degree of vibration as existence (or frequency). At ("7") we are demonstrating the uppermost ideal spiritual state of a "Being"—or else the supreme spiritual state of "*Beingness*" just outside the "Gates of the Infinite Abyss."

By definition, we cannot be certain that there is any sense or *Self-Awareness* as an "individuated spirit" or "Identity" as *Self*, even as "spirit," once we step into the "Infinity of Nothingness." There is an irony here, because although we set our sights on "*Infinity*" at ("8"), in terms of Self-Actualization as a *realization*, the *actual* goal is: a defragmented ideal clear state of *Beingness* of the "I-AM-*Self*" at (7.0). Furthermore, at *Grade III* (and a significant portion of Professional **Piloting** Procedures taught at *Grade IV*) we are applying the same "shoot-for-just-beyond-the-goal" method to **beta-defragmentation** processing, to *actualize* a clearing of energetic channels of personal ZU up to (4.0) on the "Standard Model" by emphasizing a *realization* toward *Self-direction* of WILL at (5.0).

One of the important aspects of this *Systemology* that is not always relayed due to the emphasis on the strictly "higher" levels of understanding and reasoning that the logic and math provides—particularly toward the realm of "metaphysics" and "spirituality"—there is also the matter to attend to concerning the organic physical body that we are using as a "genetic vehicle." We place a lot of emphasis on the *Self* and higher ranges of the "spirit" because we are moving away from what we have been programmed to in the past, concerning this over-identification and entrapment of existing as a "physical body." But that is not to say that the physical body should be disregarded as unimportant. We spend a considerable amount of personal time and energy getting accustomed to our vehicle in this lifetime and its foibles: its capacity during a given point of evolution on the timeline; semantics and language inherent in communications of present culture; and essentially everything and anything that is specific or unique to our *Awareness* as an *Identity* at *this* point on the timeline of planet Earth.

> Although it may be safely assumed that the "*Alpha Spirit*" ("I-AM-*Self*") carries its own supply of ZU as to exist independent of the physical body—and therefore continue on after this lifetime—it is important that we maintain our current existence (and its most optimum operating conditions) until we can maintain a ZU-frequency as *Actualized Awareness* that would enable us to travel about the spheres, "moving in and out of bodies at WILL," which is the exact point—at (5.0)—that we find an *Alpha Spirit* still very much "alive" and "individuated" on the "Standard Model" even when participation in a specific *beta-existence* ("4.0" and below) or "Physical Universe" is absent.

Δ Δ Δ Δ Δ Δ Δ

Although we are treating the "Systemology of ZU" as a higher unifying applied spiritual technology with a semantic terminology that makes it appear quite superficial to everyday life—and the tasks and obligations of maintaining a physical existence in everyday life—an acute understanding of ZU is actually very complimentary to healthy living and participation in the experiences of the Human Condition in the Physical Universe. Unlike many former "spiritual philosophies," methods and principles that support *NexGen Systemology* are not outright rejections of the "material world."

> To do so—to blatantly rebel, ignore or reject that there is a "Physical Universe" taking place around us, is to become ignorant to systems in operation that govern such, which is otherwise known in esoteric circles as "Cosmic Law."

To rebel, ignore or reject the "Cosmic Law" governing the *Game* in which we are *Players* is the most counter-productive non-survival mode of operation one can take.

We are able to demonstrate a basic relationship, at any point along the *Standard Model*, between the *substances*, *actions* and *Awareness* that is present at that degree or within the range of a particular level. Although we have continued to apply "familiar terms" to these ranges or levels of the ZU-continuum, a beginning *Seeker* should be careful in arbitrarily applying convenient terms to the philosophy and practices of *Systemology*—such as "physical," "emotional," "psychological," &tc.—until they are familiar with their "official" application as described within texts concerning the "Standard Model" (such as "*Tablets of Destiny*" and "*Crystal Clear*"). For example, we can describe interaction and communication of ZU energy at the emotional and biochemical range, particularly under the "control" of a reactive-response system inherent to the body, which we refer to as the "**Reactive Control Center**" or "RCC" at (2.0).

A communication of ZU is inherently radiated in emotional displays, but we should not confuse the emotion itself with ZU, or even the **physiological** and biochemical descriptions for the same activity. Other more commonly used semantics are accurate within limits of the paradigm used for observing these same effects; but the accuracy of material definitions only concerns the observable effects.

Rather than treating ZU directly as one or another of these systems, it might be better considered that each of these systems—and the levels they represent—are, in fact, a representation of the total capacity of the **flow** and circulation of ZU at any given point. The "health" or "status" of each level determines the nature of ZU radiating from that level; which is a factor of chained interactions with all related systems along the ZU-line. This means that while in theory, there is nothing that can happen to the physical body or genetic vehicle that could affect the *actual* quality of the "Alpha Spirit" at (7.0), this is not the only concern.

Although the "spirit" may be "untouched," the experience that the *Self* is processing is entirely based on the hardware and programming at lower levels. We are using the sensory **faculties** and biochemistry of an organic physical vehicle to experience a physical existence and we can only expect to excel at this, or be certain of it, to the extent that our tools are properly maintained and utilized.

The greater the defragmentation at physical and emotional levels, the greater the certainty at higher levels of thought activity. It does not really matter which direction we work from to resolve this equation so long as we are left with an empowered "*Self-Honest*" individual. In most instances, a *Seeker* will work with developing their personal certainty regarding each of these levels simultaneously, although it has been observed that it is easier for many to begin with the physical and emotional levels of defragmentation that incorporate aspects, facets and elements that are closer in vibration to Physical Universe continuity and are therefore more "familiar" in *beta-Awareness*.

It is easy to slight out the significance of maintaining and developing the physical body when it seems that we are working to establish levels so far and beyond what is known of the Physical Universe. This is not the correct approach. In the **standard issue** programming of the "Human Condition" too much emphasis is placed on attaching the *I-AM-Self Identity* directly to the physical body, but that does not mean we should be in the habit of neglecting or mistreating it unnecessarily. This is one of the faults behind many of the "spiritual" approaches in the past, particularly those that emphasize a "rejection" of the Physical World. However, an intelligent *Seeker* will notice that the neglect and mistreatment of a genetic vehicle out of ignorance or avoidance will actually force more **attention** and energy toward the physical body in the long run. Essentially, the *Seeker* that operates in rejection of the Physical Universe and to its governing Cosmic Law will find themselves even more entrapped by its barriers.

In order to be successful in our "spiritual work" or "Great Work" or the "Pathway" that delivers one to higher states of *Self-Actualization*, it is necessary for the *Seeker* to recognize that they are the operator of a vehicle.

> It is true that the operator is not the vehicle and should the need arise we would simply "get out" and "walk." But, we are obviously operators of this vehicles for a reason, and it remains to be the case that we should maintain the physical form until we are certain in getting us to where we want to be.

There is no guarantee that this will be equally attained by all in this lifetime, since we can see many individuals around us who have yet to even begin to chart such a journey for themselves. However, we know that certain vistas are possible for those that seek them—for those that know to seek them. It seems necessary, even momentarily, while we travels along terrain of this portion of the *Pathway*, that the education to get "through-and-out" is earned while operating this "genetic vehicle" today. For so long as we seek to conduct our "Great Work" from these forms, it is important that we do understand them—their conditions and environment—free and clear of programmed fragmentation. Only then will we really know exactly what we are dealing with.

LECTURE FOUR

. :: **THE POWER OF ZU** :: .

BASIC SYSTEMOLOGY OF GENETIC VEHICLES

When we refer to the "*genetic vehicle*" in *Systemology*, we are referring very specifically to the *living organism*—organic and genetic in nature—that constitutes the "physical body."

This "physical body" is quite *real* as the **catalyst** for experiencing physical energy and physical matter, or else, communicating physically in the Physical Universe.

Its significance is precisely this; no more or less.

It is true that many individuals that follow standard issue Human Condition programming are of the belief that "*Self*" and "body" are one and the same in exclusion to all other existence. As such, these individuals celebrate "building" the "mass" of the body—are hypnotized to all the "abilities" that may be stored in muscle memory—demonstrating the total physical glory of human function as a physical organism. Those who have not *realized* any "higher" sense of *knowingness* or *beingness* find themselves quite enamored in their duped entrapment as the "effect" of the physical systems.

There are many that have taken the position at the other end of the pendulum swing—going as far as to punish and deprive the body of its own *beingness* to follow some or another misguided attempt at "transcendence." Far better and more efficient ways exist to operate *beyond* the *beta-Awareness* of the physical body ("genetic vehicle") that do not require any mistreatment or misalignment of emotion and "**intention**" **associated** with a "physical body."

In fact, most of the experimental research in high level (graded) work for *Systemology* is geared toward these ends, and "higher" *realizations* may be achieved when a *Seeker's Awareness* is not so pointedly fixed to the physical systems and biochemical processes of the "genetic vehicle." Rather than a rejection of the "body" or any type of philosophy that treats this experience of *Life* with disdain, we have discovered those first steps toward achieving "transcendental" states involves "defragmenting" the (ZU) energy processing at "lower" levels, thereby *Self-directing* such systems to operate optimally.

I began treating the Systemology of the organic physical universe and *genetic vehicle* in discourses comprising "*Systemology—The Original Thesis*" and initial "*Reality Engineering*" lecture series—but immediately afterward, I began to focus exclusively on a pursuit of spiritual energy and spent little time relaying information regarding the "physical body" that also existed in the equation. This proved necessary to perfect an effective and workable understanding of the "Standard Model" and interactions of ZU energy along the entire continuum of existence.

Throughout our relay of a higher systemological educational, various information is presented concerning a singular "crystalline identity expression" that "peaks" or "extends" from the ALL-as-ONE. In other "esoteric" and "Mardukite" literature, the essence of this peak is known as the "Divine Spark"—but in our progressions into further Grades (including *Grade III**), the semantics more frequently applied the "Alpha Spirit"—the *actual* point of this true "I" of-and-as "*Self.*" This is a normal emphasis and direction of our progressive work: concerning *Actualization* of the "Spirit." But this speaks very little concerning the state of the "genetic vehicle" that we obviously maintain some type of **anchor** points with during this physical lifetime (incarnation), in order to maintain a singular expression of *Identity* between, as we say: "*Infinity-to-Infinity.*"

---

* Grade-III, Mardukite Systemology, Pathway to Self-Honesty; relayed in this present volume, *"Systemology—Original Thesis" "Tablets of Destiny" "Crystal Clear"* and *Complete Mardukite Master Course.*

84

The basic differentiation between states was described a decade ago in the very first "*NexGen Systemology*" discourse:*

> "In this new field of *NexGen Systemology*, we call this 'true' original *Self*, the *Alpha* or *Free* "*Spirit*." It is the first (*alpha*) point of separation—or *Life division*—of the *ALL-as-ONE*. Its own existence is not restricted (meaning "free") to the habitation and experience of corporeal *genetic vehicles*. These *vehicles* provide exactly that: an organic *vehicle* for the 'spiritual being'— the 'True' *Self*—perceived to 'inhabit' the body. From the perspective of the *Human Condition*, the existence of the *Alpha Spirit* is wholly 'energetic'; its existence is not reduced to the 'more **condensed**' and 'slower vibrations' used to construct and maintain a '*physical/material universe*' and similarly the '*material/physical body*' it uses to experience the Physical Universe."

Further in the same article, it goes on to state that direct experience of the Physical Universe requires an appropriately designed corporeal or organic body operating on a similar enough energy frequency to interact with physical systems. As a result, "bodies" or vehicles created to do this are fixed very specifically to the systematic design of "material existence" in the "Physical Universe" as governed by "Cosmic Law."

> As a "body" of "substance" in existence, these vehicles were developed as a "system" that carries its own "genetic" programming and evolutionary processes, in addition to organic consumption and growth based on nutrient processes specific to the physical environment.

These would include the ability to grow as a certain form based on **fractal**-like genetic encoding and then subsequent

---

* Drafted in 2010 while writing "*Mardukite Liber-R*," released in 2011 as "*Human, More Than Human*," reissued in "*Systemology: The Original Thesis*" 10th Anniversary anthology by Joshua Free.

processing of ZU at all levels necessary to sustain and optimize that existence—usually under the "Prime Directive" to maintain and continue *Self-existence*. "Evolution"—by definition—is a generational continuation of "survival" information for existence; and this is accomplished on all levels via a communication of energy.

Communication of ZU at low-frequency *beta-existences* may be found to stretch across a "genetic timeline" for the entire developmental evolution of a physical genetic vehicle. Once we understood that there were "programs" or "programming"—literal "genetic encoding" programs—installed as *intelligence-systems,* only then could we provide a "Standard Model" for how systems operate (in relation to ZU) presumably all the way down into the most sub-atomic and string-like vibrations of the Physical Universe.

Although there is an emphasis on the "spiritual/alpha timeline" of the *Alpha Spirit* (and its own past lives) at higher "grades" of Systemology development, it is impossible to dismiss the "genetic timeline" that is retained as *encoding* within a *genetic* databank that very much affects the function of the "genetic vehicle" based on its own "**genetic memory**."

In essence, we find that the occupation of—or associative control of—a "genetic vehicle" by an *Alpha Spirit* involves a communication of ZU between the *Actualized Awareness* of the actual *Self* and the information processing involving biochemical systems that are programmed for the cellular and organic "perspective" of the physical "genetic organism." This particular factor of differentiation seems to have escaped the notice, research and experimental practice of even those schools of thought that *do* **acknowledge** "past lives"—and "memory regression" (or other recall methods) related to the same.

Δ Δ Δ Δ Δ Δ Δ

In former, more theoretical, years of *Systemology* development, I stated the extent of what we directly considered at that time concerning a "physical organic body" as a "genetic vehicle" for the *Alpha Spirit*. The premise—first expressed in "*Systemology: Original Thesis*"—behind later developments, simply provided a differentiation between the "genetic vehicle" and the "*Alpha Spirit*," but little else on a practical level. The main objective of the short discourse was merely to demonstrate how the *Self* was "greater than" and "independent" of anything regarding the physical body—at least on a existential level of logic bordering on the spiritual (or metaphysical). As such, a *Seeker* at that time was provided with only the most concrete premise that:

> "The *genetic vehicle* is essentially an '**intermediary**' between an *Alpha Spirit* and experience of the '*physical/material universe*' and the two can become quite intertwined in the process. The *memory* and *data* of one can and will influence the perceptions and/or behavior of the other. A *perceived ailment* or some nature of *detrimental damage* to once can become devastating to existence or a progressive hindrance to the evolution of one or *both*. Unless the 'true' nature of these systems and communications of energy are unraveled and cleared, a *human being* is left to walking the earth in a state of *schizophrenic neurosis*."

A considerable amount of information, research and exploration into the "biochemical" and "genetic" nature of the Human Condition was required; which contributed to considerable delays in codifying more recent demonstrations of "*Mardukite Systemology.*" This shift in emphasis was not intended to invoke less spiritual goals, but necessarily was required for us to plot an effective "ZU-line" applicable to, and interacting as, a chain-reaction through all levels of existence—meaning all "systems" interconnected as the "Identity" of *Self* and its interactions with an environment—or a *Self-created* "duplicate" of an environment Reality (as we have also discovered the case to be).

I considered returning to my former investigations collected in notebooks filled with anything relevant from the fields of "psychology" and "physiology" and "chemical medicine" from my academic years. Of course, the more I examined this with "new eyes," the more evidence stacked up to suggest the existence and operation of a "personal system" specifically communicating ZU through a biochemical level of the "genetic vehicle."

After reviewing older "*Reality Engineering*" lecture materials again, I noticed many answers had already been *realized* in 2013 (or prior), but were never *actualized* and codified in a way that would advance a workable "Systemology." They were not treated with any practical significance at that time. Then, while preparing the new 2019 launch (or re-launch, depending on your perspective or time spent with the organization) of *Mardukite Systemology* with "*Tablets of Destiny*," it was discovered that several of the original *Nex-Gen Systemology Society* members independently arrived at many of the same conclusions while using the materials on their own during the external "developmental lull" of official Systemology literature between 2013 and 2019.

Previously lacking in a unified "Standard Model" (and total understanding of the "ZU-line"), no consistent shared paradigm existed prior to 2019 to provide a workable and effective methodology beyond theory. A considerable amount of "fluff and greyness" remained to be overcome, which is what allows *Grade-III* textbooks—such as "*Tablets of Destiny*" and "*Crystal Clear*"—to stand apart so distinctly from former communication efforts, and why they represent a particularly significant milestone: not only for our field of *Mardukite Systemology*, but for all humanity, as it coherently bridges our future with our past for the first time, and unites our understanding of the physical and spiritual in a way that has previously been considered unobtainable. Many of the fundamentals concerning the "genetic vehicle" could be found within the (currently archived) textbook associated with the original "*Reality Engineering*" lectures:

"*Reality Experience* consists of varied 'conditions of existence' (*physical*, *spiritual*, *&tc.*) interacting with varied 'conditions of being' equating to the observed '**point-of-view**' of *Self*. The sensory range specific to the *Human Condition* and its sensory parameters is specific to the 'wiring' of the *'Genetic Vehicle'*; meaning the 'physical body' (in exclusion) is limited in its own *'consciousness-awareness'* to what exists as *'physical'* stimuli—vibrations existing within that sensory range.

"Even the (external) *'physical technologies'* employed by the 'sciences' on the 'physical plane' are restricted to the same range of what is perceivable from the *actualized* point-of-view of the *Human Condition*. Even when using instruments to detect what is beneath the range of the naked eye alone, someone has to *observe* the data; someone is always *looking* behind the lens or *watching* the film. External technologies are only an extension of the *'Genetic Vehicle'* and are still subject to qualifications of the *Human Condition* to be treated as *experience*."

Prior to a standardized systematic incorporation of "ZU" (and semantics of the "ZU-line") for *Mardukite Systemology*—as an official standalone "Core" or "Grade"—our preliminary researches and experimentation referred to the spiritual extension or "alpha" **projection** of *Self* as the "Personal Identity Continuum" extending from "*Infinity-to-Infinity*" across the ALL or total actualized potentials of existence in all existences; meaning "all spheres or circles of existence." This was easily demonstrable as a theory for "higher levels" of existence; however, when related specifically to the "*genetic vehicle*" (and its systems below the ZU-frequencies of "Thought" or else the "Mind-System"), we were forced to more closely inspect this thing we call the "physical body" from a more "systemological" point-of-view.

We established the understanding that the Mind-Systems operated above the level of condensed physical energy restricted to the "body"; yet the issue remained of unifying this understanding with the "body" as its own "genetic living system" growing independent of any "specific" spiritual consciousness or operator "behind the wheel."

> If we are "spiritual beings" (or a "spiritual consciousness") using a "physical body," then what is the nature of the "physical consciousness" specific to the "genetic organism" itself? Because it would not be dependent on any one or another specific "identity" or "Self" *to be* a genetically growing organism; much like an automobile may be operated over the course of its own "lifetime" by different operators, each with their own "lifetimes." These bodies are *more than* the product of even one single lifetime as a "genetic" being following DNA (*&tc.*) and cellular evolution in each generation.

This required us taking a step back from treating the systemology of exclusively "intellectual" and "spiritual" ideals of the *Human Condition*—a breakthrough that is most evident to *Seekers* noticing the emphasis on the "biochemical" ("physio-emotional") genetic entity in the "*Tablets of Destiny*" volume.

Δ Δ Δ Δ Δ Δ

I reexamined an early premise in *Systemology* regarding "*perturbation*"—unseen influences and causes to observable effects. It was easy to demonstrate "fragmentation" as a separation from wholeness in one direction: that the *Awareness* of an individual could so wholly identify with the physical body, so as to eliminate any higher *realizations* of experience.

It also seemed that it would be possible for this to happen from the other end (or perspective point-of-view) being:

> ...that *Awareness* and "control" of the *Self*
> —the *Alpha Spirit*—could in some way also be
> "fragmented" or "blocked" from experiencing
> "clarity" all along this personal continuum of ZU.
>
> Communication of energy along the ZU-line is not
> guaranteed to be exchanged via a "*clear*" channel.

There was more to the personal system than just a "Mind" interacting and communicating between a conscious "Spirit" and a robot "Body"—and perhaps only a few individuals in the past century had caught up to this *realization*.

> It also seemed that the *Self* could actually
> be "short-circuited" out of the "Awareness-loop"
> concerning the handling of a "body"

—and when I considered my most relatively recent life-threatening incident, I was certain something else was taking place concerning these "bodies"—something that I had not perhaps placed enough attention on understanding in the past.

From 2015 onward, the legacy behind developments of this recent surge in *Systemology* comes from a more personal source of momentum and drive: entirely *Self-directed* to see this work through for personal reasons. I had already spent enough time "looking backward" along the timeline of human history and researching "south" into all dank depths and fens to reach people on various avenues—varying traditions and semantics. But this was not enough; certainly not enough to chart a future. Not even my own.

Since 2015, having completed everything that was critical to establishing "*Grade II**" for "*Mardukite Chamberlains,*" this

---

* Also called the "Mardukite Core," material collected in *"Necronomicon: The Complete Anunnaki Legacy"* by Joshua Free; particularly, additional work behind "*NexGen Systemology*" and the establishment of 21st Century "*Mardukite Zuism*" has been, and continues to be, my sole occupation of attention, discovery and experimentation behind the scenes of the "Mardukite" presence. Only recently, with release of "*Tablets of Destiny*" and "*Crystal Clear*," after nearly half of a decade following my own personal journey on this track (which still continues), did I begin to yield any worthwhile results to share and experiment with others; and once we found that "*yes, this systemology works*," I began to pass it along internally. *But the work is still ongoing.*

Meanwhile, the first phases of my own personal goals were achieved and thus my certainty elevated toward delivering, at the very least, the portion referred to as "*Grade III*." I had to chart this specific regimen of "*Self-Defragmentation*" for *myself* and for personal reasons—resulting from years of research and then my own rehabilitation immediately after the late-2015 release of my synthesis of ancient *Systemology* for a very specific "bridge project" for a group of *Mardukite Alumni* called the *Moroii ad Vitam*,[*] when a life-threatening incident (for my current beta existence anyways) occurred.

I had only recently returned to Colorado from what had turned out to be a threat on my life of a different nature entirely—a story for another time. But, the incident that really *struck* me, involved the form of an SUV-vehicle: the reality and momentum of the vehicle's mass encountered the mass of my physical form as it moved along an intersection crosswalk. The energy-matter of a mechanical vehicle violently **displaced** the energy-matter of my genetic vehicle in the same space-time of the Physical Universe. To the layman: I was struck by an truck while walking across a street.

"The Complete Anunnaki Bible" "Sumerian Religion" "Babylonian Myth & Magic" "The Complete Book of Marduk by Nabu" and *"Novem Portis: Necronomicon Revelations"* by Joshua Free.

[*] Referring to Mardukite "Liber-V" series material, available as *"Vampyre's Handbook: Secret Rites of Modern Vampires"* 5th Anniversary Collector's Edition hardcover by Joshua Free.

Although I was rushed to a hospital emergency room in an ambulance, the incident obviously did not prove to be completely fatal—since I am still here to write these words. I certainly had experienced slight **turbulence** with physical matter in this lifetime, but medically, this incident proved the most significant to date—requiring an extensive ongoing regimen of *Self-managed* "willpower" and "conviction" to remain in any condition contributory to my continued existence in this lifetime: physically, emotionally, mentally, and yes, even my own ambitions and goals for this lifetime on a spiritual level.

Having had just completed a book concerning the nature of spiritual immortality, it seemed to me that the relative time experienced on Earth to accomplish my goals might be running a bit shorter; moving a bit quicker. I would need to focus more intensely on "spiritual technology" that could actually heighten *Actualized Awareness* from this existence into the next; something that would be of actual value beyond this life. What else is truly real for the *Alpha Spirit*?

My incident and my journey was not so much about the recovery of my state of "good health." My interests regarded only the very manner in which I experienced it when it took place and was able to bring the incident to "analytical recall."[‡] Too many facets surrounding the event reminded me of obscure investigations of knowledge I had reasoned with formerly in my youth and in participation with obscure quasi-mystical organizations, but nothing prepared me for the actual experience.

In order to remain concise and relevant: there is only one important part I wish to share, of which many have had their own opinions regarding—and of which, I have found little outside of our newly restored *Systemology* paradigm to resolve to my satisfaction. The medical community speaks of stress, shock and **unconsciousness** as if it actually *knows* something to *know about* concerning these states. The truth

---

‡   Details regarding *Analytical Recall* appear in *Crystal Clear*.

is that they do not. And in working to understand more and more of this—and the relationship between *Self* and "*body*"—I discovered that the Human Condition, as a *genetic vehicle*, does actually possess its own "reactive-response encoded control center" that operates as a result of being a living organism and its own cellular structure and not directly because of the **presence** of "Self."

The physical makeup of a living organism could also be said to be composed of ZU as the living spiritual energy of its cells and so forth, but this is not the same application of the term when we specifically describe ZU as the *Actualized Awareness* of control maintained by an *Alpha Spirit*. As such, we decided to describe this portion of the "reactive mind system" as the "*Reactive Control Center*" *(RCC)* that is plotted at (2.0) on the "*Standard Model.*" The "RCC" is demonstrated as an energetic focal point or "ZU Control Center" or primary relay point on the "Personal-Identity-Continuum" ("*ZU-line*") governing the lower portion of *beta-existence*— and corresponding levels of *beta-Awareness* tied to "emotional biochemicals" and "motor responses" of the physical body.

While "processing" my incident—something I was in the practice of doing on a basic level even before officially applying further **systematized** developments directly to the field—it was strange to me that the actual moment of the incident was not stored in "*Alpha*" memory in a manner one would expect. There was no actual recollection of the collision point—only a brief second before when the front of a car-bumper was within my periphery. Afterward, the resumption of consciousness was the moment of struggling with the body to resume a movable position up and away from the situation. Yet, there was no record of the "impact" that promoted physical injury in any of my regression efforts. I found this strange, because the idea that the unconsciousness was produced by the head concussion had to be false. Unconsciousness occurred at the moment the *Self* became *Aware* that its ability to maintain an existence as "cause" was practically 100% **thwarted**—and for a brief period, it was completely withdrawn from the **circuit**. The body continued to function in accordance with its encoding, Cosmic Law and the Physical Universe until "I" resumed control of the circuit.

It may be stated with considerable honesty that events and phenomenon surrounding this incident—and the manner of my own *Self-directed* recovery—is one of the primary motivators that drove a personal interest (or resurgence of interest) into what my "original thesis" for *Systemology* and the ramification of decades of pursuits behind *Mardukite Zuism* were reaching to beyond just a "means."

Considerable untapped knowledge continues to support the solidity and certainty of our step forward as we extended our reach socially among humanity as a "spiritual movement" or "NexGen paradigm." Very recently, I have labored to provide a once premise with some continuity across the boards; something that could effectively elevate the Human Condition to new vistas of potential and a future spiritual evolution far surpassing anything that we have been led, or programmed, to believe is possible or within the proximity of our grasp.

> The time has come for each and every one of us to dissolve erroneous beliefs that hold back further *realizations* of something more or greater than what has been demonstrated to us before. It is time to shed lifetimes of complacent reactivity to bring a new solid reality to these things and accept **responsibility** and power to create the next stage of our *actualized* evolution!

LECTURE FIVE

. :: **THE MANIFESTATION OF ZU** :: .

THE PHYSICAL UNIVERSE, PART-I

Philosophies and spiritual technologies of *Mardukite Zuism* and *NexGen Systemology* are not based on a rejection of the "Physical Universe." There *are* some other esoteric meta-physical schools of thought and spiritual traditions founded on principles that run along the lines of: "the physical universe is only an illusion" or "time is not real." Such paradigms set themselves up for complete and utter entrapment in the very same systems "rejected." Rejecting these systems; giving up all power and responsibility for them; personal participation after attributing creation of their "reality" to "another source"—all of these are surefire routes to making certain that they remain *even more real* and *more solid* and outside of *Self-directed* control. This **misappropriation** of existence is experienced as a fragmentation or barrier simply as a result of false reasoning and erroneous **association**.

The Universe is *"created"*—but it is not *"unreal."*

Reality, by definition, is composed of **agreements**; and our Physical Universe is very much composed of *agreements*, which is to say *axioms* and *a-priori postulates* about what is "to be" and "not be" in accordance with "Cosmic Law," which is itself a very strong *agreement* or *postulate* put forth to govern physical energy and physical matter in physical space and acting through physical time. There is certainly no "unreality" at work *here*.

Perception and experience of the Physical Universe is entirely restricted to sensory faculties of the *Human Condition* as related to the *"genetic vehicle."* There are some that maintain that we are "inhabiting" the *Human Condition* like layers of clothing;

> —there are others that suggest we
> operate and control the *Human Condition*
> from a point *exterior* to the physical body, but
> which is maintained by "anchor points" to the body.

It may be, as we have seen on the ZU-line, that *Actualized Awareness* or a "point-of-view" from *Self* may be set at any relative state/degree of existence—either **interior** or *exterior* to the "body" and, if we are dealing with a spiritual entity, there is obviously a point-of-view that may be *Actualized* from "alpha/spiritual" states that are *exterior* to the "Physical Universe" altogether. Our current series of articles (lectures) focuses primarily on the manifestation of ZU in the Physical Universe and as it applies to the existence and function of the "*genetic vehicle.*"

"*Spiritual Life Energy*" or "*Lifeforce*"—that we identify as ZU within the *NexGen Systemology* paradigm—is present in all facets and functions of *Life-Systems* observed in the Physical Universe; which is to say, the manifestation of all *Life* as we are able to conceive it in the Physical Universe.

ZU is found in the coding of forms and patterns as the "*Seed of Life*"; ZU is found in the *Awareness* and "spiritual" *consciousness* of all *Life*; ZU is found in the very circulation and communication of energies providing *Will* and *intention* to physical motors and actions—thus ZU is found everywhere in the Physical Universe and falls only just shy of literally describing and defining the total and utter nature of *Life* itself. It can be demonstrated then, with the *Standard Model* (and/or the **semantic-set** defining *Systemology*) that the essence of ZU—as we have described it—is the quality of existence that Humanity has long sought to unify a true understanding of manifestation as *Life,* the *Universe* and *Reality.*

Physiological sciences provide adequate base knowledge for a physical understanding of the *genetic vehicle* at purely "physical" levels of understanding, earned from crude physical observation. As previously suggested: there is no direct accounting for ZU Lifeforce within *Living Systems* using calculations from material sciences—only an observation of motions and activities at physical levels of causality. This suffices for crudely understanding physical systems of the *Human Condition*, but speaks nothing of any levels above and below the range that we can directly observe. And while a physical scientist would state that these physical levels are all that is necessary in understanding the physical conditions, we know in *Systemology* that the adoption of a holistic "wide-angle" approach is the only valid one for all "levels." This, however, does not dismiss that organic systems operate specifically for the *genetic vehicle* and that these systems were arranged as "organic mechanic devices" to provide efficient automatism for the *genetic vehicle*.

Each organic system is set to function on its own, in relation to other systems that, combined, make up the total *Life-System* for the organism. On a physical level, we can only account for the organic matter and organic chemical energy that may be calculated as elements and substances of the material universe. And yet, these parts, in exclusion, do not actually make up the total qualities of the living system.

ZU-energy inherently in the "blood" is not specifically the chemical elements that may be analyzed in a physio-chemical laboratory. Yet, at the same time, and restricted to only a physical paradigm—such as "cellular biology"—we can almost just as "accurately" predict the motions and actions of *living systems* based on the "causality" that we *can* observe at a physical level, and hence why most scientific knowledge, regardless of how valid it may appear, is still treated as "theory" at the purist level of academic semantics. So long as they remain consistent and go unchallenged by any others with greater veracity, all of the theories, theorems and axiomic knowledge of former generations still continues with us today—with the most popular *agreements* generally regarded as "*fact.*"

Communication of ZU energy circulates throughout a *genet-*

ic vehicle as a type of "nerve energy"—or else the "nervous system" of the organism. Chemical processes and motors account for the "physics" of action taking place, but not the *Will-Intention* that is directing the motion. The "Mind-System"—as plotted on the *Standard Model/Zu-line*—is not the "brain" of the *genetic vehicle*, but it does directly communicate with the "brain" (physical organs) as an integral of the nervous system of the body.

We often say that there is no way an *Alpha Spirit* can be permanently affected by alterations or facets of the body, but communication with the body can be interrupted or fragmented by physical injury to these "nerve centers." On a medical level, such injuries interrupt nerve signals that are otherwise automated by various organic systems; on a *systemological* level, we know that *Awareness* of *Self* may reach and direct energy to any part of the body.

Our ability to heal, even when using conventional physical medical treatments, is still greatly determined by the *Will-Intention* of the individual and not as a guaranteed result of the external treatments alone. Medical professionals are not ignorant to the fact that it is the *patient that chooses to be or not be well*, outside of which there is nothing even the best providable care can prevent. As the cuneiform wisdom relays on "Marduk's Tablet of Destiny"—*When disaster is self-made, no one can interfere.*[*]

Δ Δ Δ Δ Δ Δ Δ

It is not my present intent to provide a full synthesis of biology, chemistry and other physiology concerning the *"genetic vehicle"* representing the *Human Condition.* Such information may be found elsewhere. This is not to say the information is not valid or significant regarding physical systems, but it is better stated by those with greater interests and education on the mechanics of those subjects. It is sufficient to say, as we have, that there are very specific

---

[*]   See *"Tablets of Destiny"* by Joshua Free.

systems with specific functions that are all developed for operation of a "*genetic vehicle*" in the manner it stands as a biological organism at present time.

At a basic level of organic function—speaking nothing of the molecules, atoms and elemental particles vibrating matter into existence—it is the "cellular level" of a biological organism that is most pertinent to *systemology*. Regardless of what organ or form the living system requires, the basic physical biological *Life Unit* is called a "cell."

Inert physical matter contains minimal energetic ZU activity. Organic physical matter contains more energetic activity because it is directly **incited** by ZU. Just as we may describe inert matter in terms of atoms and molecules, we find the same elements composing organic matter; except that the "cell" is imbued or instilled directly with ZU energy. Essentially, a "cell" is like an atom *plus* consciousness/*Awareness*. These cells concentrate and/or group together to form larger components of organic systems, just as basic atoms may compose various types of molecules. The variation of function and type is merely a matter of "degree" along the ZU-line; or else the physical space-time relationship between energy and matter.

The entire living organism has a certain coded form, as does each individual organ, although the basic "cellular unit" is virtually identical all over. [An **exoteric** philosophical analysis of such principles may be found in *Pantheisticon*,[‡] a brief volume penned by an early proto-*systemologist*—before the term even held a meaning in the academic community[∞]—

named John Toland, an early pioneer of the 18th century Druid revival in England. To remain economical, there is no reason to duplicate this information here.] Genetic encoding allows, for example, the cells of the lungs *to be* cells of a lung organ and grow and divide (reproduce) exclusively within that system, of that type, and to perform that function. It *knows* to do this and how. We are not necessarily required to consciously direct the ZU taken in from air, water and food, or disperse it intentionally to each system, nor command cells of each system to continue their activity and reproduction. This entire sequence of information has been careful encoded into the genetic organism; it may be adaptable, but it is certainly not accidental. Many individuals have discovered that *Self* may **assume** more conscious control of these mechanistic-systems than traditionally believed.

In the academic field of "**General Systemology**," the *genetic vehicle*—any "living organism"—is treated as an "open system." On a spiritual level (in *Systemology*), the energies directed from *Self* are represented with the symbol for "alpha," which is an "open" infinity-loop, or "open string." In contrast, each universe is existentially treated as a "closed system" independent of other theoretical universes.

We use the "b" to represent *Self* in "beta" as the descent of energy into a closed loop. But this simply demonstrates a creative use of symbols. A universe is a **singularity** or **continuity**. The symbols are meant to represent ZU, not the environment, because we calculate for a transmission of ZU energy through this universe that comes from and goes out to an existence that is *exterior* to this one. The only equations where this is a factor in the Physical Universe all relate to ZU or "*Spiritual Life Energy*."

---

and ludology (concerning the Human Condition). Incorporation of the "Arcane Tablets" and other cuneiform sources generates the flavor or paradigm known as "*Mardukite Systemology*" for *Grade-III* (as introduced in "*Tablets of Destiny*").

In our *Systemology*, we are treating all aspects holistically, and so this information is not even a surprise; it is directly "predicted" by the *Standard Model/Zu-line*. Yet, even on a purely physical level, we can treat the *genetic vehicle* as an "open system" and be semantically correct, as explained by Ludwig von Bertalanffy in his famous treatise on "<u>General Systems Theory</u>":—

> "We realize at once, however, that there may be systems in equilibrium in the organism, but that the organism as such cannot be considered as an equilibrium system.
>
> "The organism is not a closed, but an open system. We term a system 'closed' if no material enters or leaves it; it is called 'open' if there is import and export of material.
>
> "There is, therefore, a fundamental contrast between chemical *equilibria* and the metabolizing organisms. The organism is not a **static** system closed to the outside and always containing the identical components; it is an open system in a (quasi-)steady state, maintained constant in its mass relations in a continuous change of component material and energies, in which material continually enters from, and leaves into, the outside environment."

We could take a purely materialist approach and apply a "*Life*" quality to "living organisms" only in regard to the consumption and waste of material "energy." With exception to organic processes, the entire field of physical sciences were treated as a "closed system" and entirely mechanistic. This is why the elemental and chemical sciences seem so cold and unfeeling—they are treating the Physical Universe at its lowest possible frequencies and conditions of solidarity. Even these are said to be "alive" and buzzing with electronic and atomic motion at the more fundamental levels of existence. When we say that "everything is in motion" *we mean* "everything is in motion." Even what is called inert matter still maintains some nature of vibration for it register in existence. The symbol of "zero" used to represent such continuity is, for our purposes, a "theoretical construct."

Principles of ZU as *Life* are demonstrated of a different nature than these other "closed systems." It may be the case, at the highest level of order, that these "open systems" of *Life* in the Physical Universe are actually "closed systems" in a wider more encompassing existence (such as *Infinity*), but for understanding how *Life* interacts in the Physical Universe: it is an "open system" in an otherwise "closed system." ZU as *Life* may be the *only true* "open system" extant in the Physical Universe. We represent the Physical Universe as a "closed system" continuity of "inert" elemental/material (substance) with the symbol "*Zero*" (in higher treatments of *Systemology*), which relates to another statement made by Ludwig von Bertalanffy:—

> "A closed system in equilibrium does not need energy for its preservation, nor can energy be obtained from it. For example, a closed reservoir contains a large amount of (potential) energy; but it cannot drive a motor. The same is true of a chemical system in equilibrium. It is not a state of chemical rest; rather reactions are continually going on, so regulated by the law of mass action that as much is formed of every species of molecules or ions as disappears. Nevertheless, the chemical equilibrium is incapable of performing work. For maintaining the processes going on, no work is required nor can work be won from It. The algebraic sum of work obtained from and used by the elementary reactions equals *zero*."

Δ Δ Δ Δ Δ Δ

Personal energy is expended in the basic biological processes—all of which are circulating ZU—even if they are concentrated as mechanical-like automation that does not require significant attention by *Self* in order to function.

Rest assured that the design is a result of *some* Alpha Spirit's creation—one that, somewhere back on the timeline, contributed to the inception of this very specific *genetic form* for the *Human Condition*. Our *Systemology* demonstrates that ZU is entered into the system from the Spiritual Universe as *Self-directed* by, or at least from the direction of, the "*Alpha Spirit.*" Our model demonstrates that "personal fragmentation" causes **turbulence** and restriction to free circulation of ZU through *Life-systems* of an organism.

Depletion of energy that is otherwise consumed by natural organic processes and motors is easily replaced by its being fed into the system with the full vitality and optimum levels of operation at high frequencies. This does not mean that *Systemology* is a physical "cure-all"—even if it was, we could never suggest it so—*but* we may demonstrate that states of *defragmentation* and high frequency ZU promote conditions for optimum physical health, which may be maintained and supplemented by appropriate physical routines that are preventative measures. We are interested in maintaining good health because physical systems of the *Human Condition* are interconnected with the "spiritual systems" and our *Awareness* to direct the power of ZU.

> In *Systemology*, the ZU-line is treated as a continuous *flow-line* from "source"—whatever relay point that may be. It flows, undoubtedly, by definition, from the "ABZU" as a "source." Once formed, the point of the *Alpha Spirit* (plotted at "7.0" on the *Standard Model*) becomes a "source" as *Self*. The ZU directed from *Self* is concentrated again at the threshold between the "Spiritual" (AN) and "Physical" (KI) at the "Mind-System"—where the "*Master Control Center*" (MCC) is treated as a "source" of ZU for the *beta-Awareness* of a living organism.

The flow of ZU energy—along the "ZU-line"—is a systematic relay between points that trade off roles: sometimes as the "effect" of a "higher" order of ZU communication; then as the "source" of this continued transmission to "lower" processes. The optimization of this system is not toward efficiency in establishing an equilibrium state, but rather a promotion of continuous flow of ZU throughout, un-**inhibited** and unrestricted by fragmentation. Ludwig von Bertalanffy explicitly explains this quality of "flow" as the difference between the latent potential of a "closed system" and the active energy potentials of "open systems":—

> "In order to perform work, it is necessary that the system be not in a state of equilibrium but tend to attain it; only then can energy he won. In order that this is achieved continually, the hydrodynamic as well as chemical system must be arranged as stationary—*i.e.*, a steady flow of water or chemical substances must be maintained whose energy content is transformed into work. Continuous working capacity is, therefore, not possible in a closed system which tends to attain equilibrium as soon as possible, but only in an open system. The apparent 'equilibrium' found in an organism is not a true equilibrium incapable of performing work; rather it is a '**dynamic** pseudo-equilibrium', kept constant at a certain distance from true equilibrium; so being **capable** of performing work but, on the other hand, requiring continuous import of energy for maintaining the distance from true equilibrium."

An example of "Energy work" pertaining to this same flow of personal ZU is demonstrated in a previous volume referring to circulation of such energies as *Starfyre.** Circulation of personal energy promotes the processes necessary for "healthy growth" or "continuation," which is described in *Systemology* as the "Prime Directive"—the fundamental principle driving existence *to exist*. In most cases, additional instruction on this subject is not necessary for a *Grade-III* student of the *Mardukite Systemology Core*.

---

* See *"The Vampyre Handbook"* by Joshua Free.

However, this application to the "physical everyday world" is important if we are to maintain a coherent context for *Systemology* as effective and relevant for the *Human Condition* at its current state on the timeline. Present efforts to transmit this information is a necessarily condition for enhancing and accelerating positive movement of the *Human Condition* through to its next evolution as a species—one that we have referred to in *Systemology* very specifically as the **metahuman** state of "***Homo Novus.***"

But, what is it that promotes a physical *and* spiritual evolution toward this new *actualized* condition for the *Actualized Awareness* governing the *genetic vehicle*?

Given that the supply of ZU is a constant from its *Alpha* state, then short of dealing with high frequency "alpha defragmentation," the most important application of *Will* and *Intention* in *beta-existence* is "beta defragmentation"—such as is introduced in the primary *Grade-III* textbooks: "*Tablets of Destiny*" and "*Crystal Clear*." The reason for this is that it increases the amount of *Actualized Awareness* (ZU) circulating through the *genetic vehicle* and thereby contributing to its optimum operation. Natural adaptation to a higher capacity of ZU may already be taking place among the recent generations of *genetic vehicles* based on external influences that have yet to be fully understood. In any case, the individual (reading this book)—or a *Seeker* on the *Pathway to Self-Honesty*—is in a position to increase their personal circulation of ZU energy and, as such, increase the presence of this vital cosmic energy in everyday living.

> With an increase of ZU follows increased efficiency of *livingness*; increased power; increased success; and we would assume that if you are playing the *Game* properly, increased happiness and enthusiasm toward the future potential of *Life,* the *Universe* and *Everything!*

LECTURE SIX

. :: **THE ELEMENTS OF ZU** :: .

THE PHYSICAL UNIVERSE, PART-II

In some mystic philosophies, it would be sufficient to state that "ZU" (or its *approximated equivalent*) is "ZU" and leave it at that. Of course, other mystic philosophies do not ascribe to themselves the title: *systemology.* We are concerned with "high thought" and intellectual analysis of reasoning that is now so "second nature" and "automated" that we have a generation of individuals questioning the very holographic reality of their universe. And rightly so.

> We should always *seek* the highest understanding we can attribute to our experiences—so long as they are "true experiences" in *Self-Honesty.*
>
> –If you *cannot* be absolutely certain of the nature of experience, the only solution is the *Pathway to Self-Honesty.*
>
> –If you *do* feel absolutely certain of your experience and your programming, then you should find *NexGen Systemology* and the bulk of what is behind *Mardukite Zuism* is more of a confirmation and solidarity of truth with *systematic* vocabulary rather than an indoctrination into some newfangled religion of novel fancy.

Certainly: ZU is ZU; ZU is ZU all along the ZU-line. A little hint here: *it is why* we call it a *"ZU-line."* It is a continuum of a singularity that differs in degree as its only point of *variation.* Different combinations of this singularity as a manifestation—combining its degree with its environment or conditions—results in various types, flavors, or species of variation. The fundamental and most basic principle essence is still ZU, in whatever aspect it is being treated. For example: there is a necessity for the *"genetic vehicle"* to consume fuel in order to operate. But we are not treating an arbitrary "closed system" consumption of fuel, such as when we burn a log on a fire. ZU is present in such manifestations and processes of the Physical Universe too, just not of the same *type* as when we treat ZU as a *Spiritual Lifeforce* (such as we find in all vital organic existences); nor is it the same *type* as the ZU present in the *Seed of Life* that encodes all manifest existences—or at the very least, all manifest existences present in the Physical Universe.

Some individuals (examining these present articles) might wonder why any attention is given to these rudimentary aspects of physical existence—and living in that existence. You might think I have a low opinion of the *Human Condition* and that all individuals require education and drilling in how to live, exist and continue that existence? Obviously, not—since the *Human Condition* successfully crawled to "make it this far" with random "hit and miss" approaches to experience. But, have we really made it so "far"? If this "hit and miss" method of *livingness* is bringing us to a point where we must literally "evolve or die" then it cannot be working very well—no matter how much we *self-hypnotize* ourselves in false acceptance to the "way things are," succumbing to complacency and agreeing to a reality for the sake of some erroneous material ideal, when we actually know better. How long is it realistic to expect existence to continue on this track and still support any *livingness*?

An individual can usually get along through several decades of existence controlling a single *genetic vehicle* through, what is considered, an "average lifespan" on purely low-level physical knowledge; such as you would receive by general societal indoctrination. There is no disputing this. Of course, this speaks nothing of the happiness or quality of *livingness* experienced, or the true range that is otherwise possible. An individual can even be kept alive "imprisoned" for the duration of an "average lifespan."

There is no general education offered concerning "best practices." We cannot even be sure if supposed authorities even maintain any kind of *reality* on the "best practices" then alone be left to wonder why such information cannot be shared freely with all equally—but evolution, it seems, has never been equal. Monkeys stayed monkeys. *Homo Erectus* replaced *Homo Habilis* and then were replaced themselves. They did not evolve to **Homo Sapiens**. At best they may have reached *Neandertal*. Even still: *Neandertal* and *Homo Sapiens* once cohabited on the timeline... only one became *Homo Sapiens Sapiens*. The other did not evolve at all. The other did not earn the *Awareness* necessary to continue an existence. And here we are now:

Homo Sapiens Sapiens versus the coming race, *Homo Novus*.
Only one will survive.

We all sense there is a *better way*; a "higher route" to travel and achieve a higher state of *beingness*. Unfortunately, there have been very few through-way avenues to grant the *Human Condition* any gain in this direction. But, very fortunately, there are at least a few of us today still here, alive and kicking alongside you, working to *actualize* an *Awareness* of a "better world" right now. And it is very possible. It is happening. And it begins with a healthy and strong individual. A strong movement—a strong organization—requires a strong and healthy individual. So, that is what I am here promoting or introducing in this brief series of articles (lectures).

There are some that dismiss these rudiments as unimportant, but they are not. Additionally, we must be absolutely certain that *Seekers* have found and achieved the solid footing available at *Grade III* (demonstrated here and in "*Tablets of Destiny*" and "*Crystal Clear*") before advancing ahead on the *Pathway*, even though the material only seems to get more and more "interesting" the further we go. The work is, however, only as practical as the extent it may be used, and hence why I have decided to review these present topics before officially moving work any further in published form.

We are now, already, in the midst of the *Third Gate* at *Grade III Mardukite Systemology*, and there is no substitute for an appropriate level of *Self-Honesty* once a *Seeker* seeks passage beyond this point.

We aren't demanding perfection from you at this point. We aren't asking for a game-ending win. We are saying that we can all do just a bit better. And after that. A little more. We are taking steps. We are relying on **sure-footing** to carry to the next threshold.

It may be generally stated that the standard issue instruction and methods of operating the *Human Condition* do not provide the most efficient optimum results—and certainly provide no guarantees as a catalyst to a higher order of *knowingness* and *beingness*. The ZU flows in on the line at a constant; free-flowing ZU energy is abundant in existence. Therefore, the main low-level obstructions to *clear vision* of *Self-Honest* reality experience must then pertain to "wasted" energy; other specific uses of personal ZU as *beta-Awareness*; and replenishing ZU in *beta-existence* via defragmented channels or conduits. This relates to any communication of (ZU) energy along any line.

In regards to the *Human Condition* operating as an "open system" of *Spiritual Life Energy* (ZU): the conditions specifically pertaining to the *genetic vehicle* are treated in other mystical, spiritual and philosophic paradigms as "The Elements." Using semantics from such paths, ZU is the quintessence of all individual elements, or else "*Akasha.*" It is the spiritual element and quality that is within all existence—the great "cosmic energy" or "universal agent" that the mystic-priest and wizard-magician also seeks. It is possible, in theory, that this inherent ZU in all existence—that the "**pantheist**" has come to consider "Divine"—is actually the residual essence remaining to keep "material" and "substance" in existence as space in time, once put forth by the *Alpha Spirit* (or *Spirits*) that designed this present rendition of the Physical Universe. This is then reinforced by our participation by agreement with said Universe following the lines of the "Observer Effect." I am merely putting this forth as conjecture at this time; something for consideration.

Δ Δ Δ Δ Δ Δ Δ

If we examine the "Elemental Model" most widely adopted in esoteric philosophies: *earth* is equivalent to the substance or food that we process; *water* is... water; and *air*... well, the systemology behind organic processing is practically self-explanatory. A *genetic vehicle* is something of a carbon-oxygen heat-generator: the transformative *fire* that consumes, processes and wastes the sustenance from these other elements. But it is ZU that provides these manifestations with their qualities as *Life-sustaining Energy*, without which we would not earn any nourishment.

Iron and lead are both substances manifesting in similar type, yet iron contains more ZU and is present in our blood. It may actually be beneficial for the *organism* to replenish it in small doses—particularly females, which lose iron in menstrual blood. On the other hand too much iron is deadly. As a substance, its mass and volume cannot replace the equivalent of other food types. And lead is toxic, in high doses, but also a cumulative toxin stored in the body—which diminishes its ability to process other nutrients.

So, while we may speak philosophically of "*unification*" and treat the ZU-line as a "singularity" of the true Cosmic Energy, we can see that in a world of manifestations: all things are not equal to all things. Things in the Physical Universe have type and variety that contributes to an observed quality. Many of these qualities and significances are not absolutes and are appropriated specifically by an individual's *Awareness.* This quality of physical energy and matter may or may not be easily quantified—for example, on the *Standard Model*—but it is still a variation in degree that we may observe real enough to treat "things in exclusion to other things." There is no great philosophical issue for this in a world of forms, because without it: where does a "table" end and a "floor" begin?

I have no reason to put forth a series of complications or metaphysical word-play. There is no reason to throw ourselves into some total superficial nihilistic approach to the Physical Universe. We can assume we are in part, responsible for part of this universe, and a participation in "things" being what "things are." And the more we can take *Self-Honest* responsibility[*] for, the greater a reach we may extend *to be* the "cause" of the "change that we want to see" actualized in this world.

If a *Seeker* examines—or perhaps has already examined—preliminary instruction regarding all basic spiritual, mystical, magical or metaphysical processes developed by other paradigms along the historical timeline of humanity, they will relate back to the "Elements" in some way or another; including a methodology of "energy work" or means of "creative processing" that familiarizes a *Seeker* with streams or rays connected to "elemental forces" of Nature. Additionally, a *Seeker*—or "initiate"—is instructed in the "proper manner" of managing personal energy reception and projection, including the (ZU) energy inherent within the *foods*, *water* and *air* that we are consistently processing to maintain functionality of a *genetic body*. We cannot deny that while each individual carries their own tendencies and preferences, there actually are "best practices" for each. Fragments of this knowledge is too often demonstrated more "mysteriously" than it actually is—appearing frequently in such discourses as regarding the "*magic of water*" or "*spiritual energy of breathing,*" &tc.

I have stated—in other lectures and writings—that preliminaries of personal development, no matter what mystic or "New Thought" tradition they are pulled from, are too often overlooked by the average *Seeker* that is always searching for something "brighter" and more "colorful"; something

---

[*]   This subject is treated further in *"Crystal Clear."*

that will produce the objective "fireworks" that blows up the truth behind the curtain. It pains me to tell you this: but at no point do I expect you to "sprout wings" from this material. The very fact that we should have to pause and discuss the basic functions of the *Human Condition* demonstrates that this material represents the first step toward brighter things. How evolved is an individual dismissing the significance regarding "conscious reception of ZU" as the *Lifeforce* and *Vital Spiritual Energy* imbuing *Life* with *Life*—and contributing to a continuation of *Life?*

Then, you tell me: "Well, I already know how to eat, drink and breathe. So, this is ridiculous." Alright, I am going to say this one thing that cannot be overstated:

> *All* individuals believe themselves to be in possession of as much reasoning as is necessary to survive. An individual is inclined, whether from millions of years of *genetic* programming and/or other **emotional encoding** of *this* lifetime, to *be, think* and *perform* as they do. Seldom does the *true Alpha personality* of the individual even have a chance to shine through with all of the fragmentation standing in the way. Usually an individual is not even *Aware* that their true **personality** is being displaced.

More to the point: an individual of the standard issue variety is not given adequate instruction on the manner of which the *Human Condition* actually functions. This may be due to some ulterior purposes of control by an upper **echelon** authority level; one that keeps individuals attributing "source-cause" to anything other than *Self* in order to make the "real" even "more real" and keep it from being handled properly by any one individual or group. Of course, it may also be due to sheer ignorance—since most "common sense" of yesteryear has ceased to be common and is now treated as some mystical supernatural "wizard sense." Then again, I suppose, if we contrast these two states of, or approaches to, operating the *Human Condition*: being in the *know* might actually seem pretty "*magical*" to the *other* folk.

Initiates and novitiates of esoteric and arcane arts receive instruction for "conscious reception of energy" from foods we eat, water we drink, and air we breathe. When we consider how closely the *Pathway to Self-Honesty* mirrors similar models—such as the "Basic Human Needs" or "Pyramid of Self-Actualization" &tc.—we should not be surprised that fundamentals of *livingness* should be found in mastery of *having* our *genetic vehicle* in optimum operation. This includes proper maintenance of the body to reach the ends that acquisition of this physical form is not burdensome in this *Lifetime*, and therefore an additional source of *fragmentation* to hinder our progress up, out and beyond these forms. The more *Awareness* an individual must fix on remedying and repairing the *genetic vehicle*, the less it may be applied to higher endeavors.

Therefore, it makes logical sense that we should find the ways that provide most efficient processing of ZU through the physical body.

True mystical masters, spiritual leaders, effective philosophers and Ascended Ones have all left a visible trail in their wake. Here we are, over the course of 6,000 years since the proto-Sumerian inception of the current civilization—and over 4,000 years since the systematization of the Mardukite Standard in Babylon, whereby humanity received programming with "language"—we are in a position to experiment with, synthesize and *know* a great deal from our past. This has been a primary task of the modern *Mardukite Systemology* movement, but only to the degree that it is effective, workable and improves the conditions of *Life* for the future spiritual evolution of *Humanity*—a continuance of the ability to exist at the most ideal states attainable for the *Human Condtion*, which is milestones ahead of where we find the general population today. But, we are taking baby-steps. And that means: not missing steps. So, here we are previewing the fundamentals; making certain that nothing has been overlooked at this way-station before charging ahead on the *Pathway*.

We could derive a considerable amount of material for *Systemology* regarding these subjects, but this would be a **repetitive** return to our emphasis on *Actualized Awareness* stated elsewhere. A greater level of *Awareness* is simply applied particularly to "conscious reception of ZU." There is nothing obscure or wrong with imbuing intention onto the sustenance that is to be consumed; the idea of blessing or praying over food and water—charging it with the highest ideal—is not restricted to any one or another tradition on the timeline. The other point-of-fact we might note, regarding those individuals that were successful on this track in the distant past, is the manner of consumption. These individuals were not gluttons and did not treat the body with excess. In fact, we have found that more "enlightened" individuals actually consume less physical matter and yet absorb more ZU. That's interesting. So, it is not the quantity that causes us to sustain or starve; and it may not be restricted to just the quality of one's diet either—although natural foods; grains; rice; seeds; nuts; olive oils; fruits; the foodstuffs that retain the unprocessed "qualities of life" all carry a higher capacity of ZU.

Significant attention given to health regimens in this commercial society has come to border on the "trendy" and "faddish." This only furthers a separation between what is "best practices" and what is simply "elitism." It has gotten to where many are convinced that "healthy living" is somehow "more" expensive in the long-run—and perhaps in many ways it is marketed as such, since there seems to always be a social tendency to try and preserve the "rich" and "political leaders" and treat working classes as a disposable battery. This is not as strictly evident in the most ancient civilizations, but we certainly see a rise of it **correlate** with the industrial mechanization of society as we come closer to the present on the timeline.

Many leaders have most likely experienced brainwashing into assuming that "the way things are" is "the way things are" and this is what they are put in charge of enforcing the solidarity of: to keep things "the way they are." This is no less found in the academic community—one that does not permit an original thought until perhaps partially sometime near a point where the student is forced to develop a doctoral thesis; but even then, every statement of "fact" must be attributed to someone else, some other source. The student is not permitted to independently arrive at any conclusions that may duplicate a cognition already one held, or many times, in the past or documented as such and so forth. But this is not the point of our present article.

We know that ancient mystics and distant yogis were all very *light* consumers. This promoted healthier and more vibrant personal energy systems—not only specific to organic mechanics of the *genetic vehicle*, but also to keep channels clear for energetic distribution and communication of *Awareness*. Tools are only effective to the degree which they are "sound" and maintained functional, in addition to skills of the operator utilizing them.

It has been suggested in numerous arcane and esoteric sources that a *Seeker* should not overwhelm their biological system with excessive food—and that all food taken in should be properly broken down in the mouth before swallowed. At best, we may determine that a greater amount of ZU may be received from high-energy foods by reducing materials to the smallest finest parts—even into a pasty mush—prior to introduction to the digestive system. An entire **eastern** philosophy developed around metabolism and the heat properties of foods and such, but really, the greater *Actualized Awareness* applied to the Physical Universe, the more aptly, able and likely an individual is to apply "best practices" to their *livingness* factor.

We might apply the same basic idea to the *water* we drink; which is actually an even more famous "mystical" example than treating the energy of "food." Many spiritual traditions maintain beliefs about qualities of water; particularly the fact that it is the most "receptive" Element, and thus easy to "**charge**" with intention. The very physical composition of water itself is also fundamentally critical to the type of organic lifeform used for a *genetic vehicle*. There are numerous mythological paradigms and spiritual systems that even identify "water" as the most perfected icon or symbolic representation of *"Life."*

It is critical to remain hydrated but not to the point of engorging the system with excess fluid. Excess of any kind contributes to states of "heavy" energy, which is usually due to the unnecessarily excessive "waste processing" that is required—which actually can consume more ZU energy than is received when dietary regimens or intake habits are not optimum. Similar beliefs are maintained by followers of the *Old Schools* concerning reception of ZU while food and water is broken down in the mouth and its dispersal once sent to the stomach.

It is not the intention of this article to imply a particular philosophy or ethic regarding the type and handling of foods and sustenance. As an individual increases in their *Actualized Awareness*, certain facets pertaining to nutrition and physical well-being should become clearer as personal patterns are observed. The intention of *NexGen Systemology* is not to impose one or another fact as to *what* to think or do—except in regards to knowing *how* to think "holistically" and "systematically" in wider and more largely encompassing ways that are not generally *realized* in the standard issue programming of the *Human Condition*. Our purpose is to redefine, expand and advance what it means to be a NexGen "next spiritual evolution" *Human*: the state of *Homo Novus* which is possible to achieve in this lifetime.

LECTURE SEVEN

. :: **THE BREATH OF LIFE** :: .

ENERGY OF ZU IN AIR AND SPACE

In a previous chapter (lesson), we introduced the spiritual properties of ZU as present in all "mystical" and "chemical" Elements. There is *one* deserving of a special article on its own, of which we will treat here. This is specifically the Element of AIR. And this Element means different things to different people. On one hand, we have a physical scientist or physician that treats "air" we breathe—and processes of breathing—as nothing more than a significant and necessary automatic function used to distribute oxygen through the body. Given our general tolerance band in *NexGen Systemology* for the semantics of various systematic "levels," we might agree that within the paradigm of physiology, the air we breathe is very much a necessary process to maintaining proper circulation of *Lifeforce* in the body—however that *Lifeforce* might be treated or labeled in some arbitrary paradigm. One scientist calls it *oxygen*. Another calls it *blood*. Chemists refer to mixtures of *carbon* and *hydrogen*. We have certainly found no shortage of ways of separating and labeling the forms and functions of whatever we can perceive in and of the Physical Universe.

Another consideration for us—beyond a dependency on "air" as the oxygen we breathe—is the property called "*pressure*." Even putting aside necessary dietary sustenance for the "body" found in other Elements, the *genetic vehicle* is only designed to exist within a very fixed parameter of air *pressure*. It is not even given free movement within the totality of the Earth sphere; suffocating itself with incredible discomfort if sent too high above or too far below the "*terran*" surface. This is only a minor consideration until we realize that these *genetic vehicles* were meant to stay here on Earth; something external technologies don't actually compensate for.

> The *Human Condition* would have to be, at the minimum, *beta-Actualized* to even begin to cope with psychological and spiritual facets of "Space" beyond Earth; and this says nothing of the physical limitations of the "genetic vehicle."

It is the *Self* or *Alpha Spirit* that is really permitted any possible freedom from the terrestrial chains once *Actualized Awareness* is *defragmented* up into that "source-point." The Human Condition seems a long way off from that state—based perhaps on current descriptions in this series of articles—and yet the truth of the matter is, although we have much ground to cover ahead on higher Grades of the *Pathway*, there is really *no* distance at all—and it needs not be some long arduous journey to accomplish, so long as we proceed with determination and certainty until we have returned the full determination and certainty to *Self* in order *to be*. Once we have cleared the way to these states, it becomes **successively** easier each time to achieve and maintain them. The Masters have told us at the end of their own journeys that it "may be realized in a single breath"—within *one* single *Self-directed* moment *to be*. We have *realized* the *Pathway*; we are now simply working our way to *actualize that moment.*

The composition of "air" on Earth—and what the chemist will describe in terms of carbon and hydrogen and oxygen—makes it a premium receptor for ZU energy. Qualities of "air" and "ZU" share greater **affinity** in the Physical Universe than any other Element. In one sense, it is the ZU within air that is imbued in the "earth-foods" that are consumed; and chemically, it may be very easily associated with "water." Even combustion and transformation of "fire" requires the "air," which is also to say "space," in order to conduct its processes. In relation specifically to organic processes of the *genetic vehicle*: proper circulation—or oxygenation—of the body most often corresponds with positive circulation of ZU energy. I am not about to put forth speculation about *how* one affects the other because at each level of semantics, paradigms or literal understanding, an individual is usually inclined to refer to the *source* as one finite point or another.

The chemist or nutritionist can use a vocabulary describing various types and degrees of elements and minerals in food, water and air; the physicist speaks in terms of particles and the transformation of energies; and so on—but none of these paradigms conclusively refers to a true *source-point*, nor are they interested in holistically combining their understandings into a general paradigm called "Life" or "The Way"—and so at times it seems as though each paradigm is essentially describing a completely different universe.

A *NexGen Systemologist* or *Mardukite Systemologist* is educated to investigate this thing called *cosmic ordering* back of all existences holistically—and this is what causes us to treat the fundamental philosophies of this pursuit as a science—

> a new *NexGen* science—whereby we may establish
> an understanding that isn't dependent on citation
> of investigations from our predecessors.

There are others that are a little less interested in the theoretical philosophy and have taken up this science *on faith* simply because it *is* effective and so we acknowledge the tradition of *Mardukite Zuism* also as a religion *of faith*, rooted in ancient Mardukite Babylonian systemology and the original systematized "Anunnaki Religion" of Mesopotamia.

Collectively, with this new paradigm set forth, the universe is *ours* to rediscover, take responsibility for, and "name" as our own creation. Only then do we exercise *true power*. This is a state of *Self-Honesty* realized in *this* lifetime, whereby freedoms of the *Spirit* are rehabilitated. As we develop more and more responsibility and certainty for our *Self-direction*, the ability automatically follows. This ability has never diminished, really. It is the *Actualized Awareness* that has been dimmed or clouded with obstruction. A parallel may easily be drawn concerning absorption of ZU and oxygen in the *genetic vehicle*—concerning the flow, the delivery, the obstructions or potential restrictions possible; all of these are applicable examples for oxygen *and* ZU in the organism.

Whether introduced in "meditation exercises," "creative visualization" or other methods of "mysticism" and "spirituality," we always find the subject of "Breathing" treated among preliminaries. This is again frequently overlooked by an initiate, because the common assumption is simple: "We all breathe; we are always breathing; what is the point of giving this any significance?" This is the very reason for the current series of articles, because before I can comfortably deliver the work officially forward to higher Grades with any certainty, it is important that these remedial points of fact are taken into account—and certainly such attitudes have been reevaluated with *Self-Honesty*.

Whenever we begin to treat the *significance* of the most obvious steps on the *Pathway* as anything less, there is a risk to skidding across a slippery slope that will deliver us nowhere or slumped back against the fragmented states from which we came. The same may be said of an individual's allergy to "semantics"—the sighs and moans over instruction of definitions and other such "boring" things. As soon as this attitude or belief enters the picture, then everything becomes *meaningless*—at least as literal communication.

> If "words" cannot be demonstrated to *mean what they mean* as a literal "symbol" of *A-for-A*, then any use of them to convey communication is equally meaningless; it will not carry the true meaning intended, nor its corresponding energy.

And it would be impossible to provide this solid foundation of knowledge as a spiritual philosophy or NexGen science without a pointedly clearly defined semantic baseline for communication. The preliminaries of this application are no different. The basic fundamentals in *Self-direction*, *Will* and *Intention*—that are common to all traditions extending from the Ancient Mystery School—cannot be overlooked if a

Seeker intends to share a genuine energetic communication with what "symbols" represent. And this applies to all paradigms; not only *Systemology*.

Δ Δ Δ Δ Δ Δ

Let us say, for the sake of physical continuity, that oxygen is of such a type that it carries or transmits ZU energy throughout the *genetic vehicle*. When we speak of energy circulation; messenger-carriers; **wave** actions; motions; communication in general—we are necessarily calling up what the old mystic described as the functions of the Air Element: often represented by symbols of the breath; the wind; the wand; wing and feather; the pen, quill and stylus; the voice; the sound; the space within and without solids; the light-sight particle-waves; the entire EM-electromagnetic spectrum; the thought transmission, the etheric or astral *Self*. We are running very close to actually defining ZU and *Awareness* when we touch on the Air Element. Since we can draw parallels between ZU and all Elements and Lifeforms, perhaps it would be more correct to state that: our interests in *Systemology* and the manner by which we may understand and control the power of ZU are simply best reflected by the Air Element in its relationship between the *Alpha Spirit* and the *Genetic Vehicle*—because that relationship is only maintained as a result of ZU and specifically the "Mind-System"; which would again bring us back to a "metaphysical domain" of AIR.

The Mind-System and the "Breath" are directly linked; and since we have demonstrated in the textbooks *Tablets of Destiny* and *Crystal Clear* the exact manner in which this Mind-System interacts between the *Alpha Spirit "I-AM-Self"* and the function, sensory experience and memory of the *genetic vehicle*. If a *Seeker* fully examines the systematic relay described here *Self-Honestly*—just concerning this uppermost consideration of ZU and "Air"—the individual will eventual arrive at some semblance of the "ZU-line" on their own; and thus how *we* arrived at these conclusions.

[Handout facsimile shown here.]

FIRST (ALPHA) PHASE
[Specific to the Spiritual Universe]
Alpha Spirit → **Alpha Thought** → Will-Intention

MESSENGER-ACTION / PERTURBATION
[Threshold between Spiritual and Physical Universe]
Will/Intention → (to *Genetic Vehicle*) "Mind-System"

SECOND (BETA) PHASE
[Specific to the Physical Universe]
Mind-System → Beta-Thought → Effort/Emotion → Result

It is an interesting observation that many individuals believe that breathing is regulated solely on automatic programming. Although it is true that there is a program set forth by the nervous system to gauge rhythm, the entire manner by which one is accustomed to breathing is conditioned, either by one or another facet of genetically coded memory, or by proper training and *Self-direction*. An individual can condition the body to change the manner in which it regulates circulation of oxygen in the system. And this is very interesting to a *Systemologist* that is learning about proper systematic control of the body. If circulation of oxygen-carrying-ZU is critical to optimum operation of all functions of the *genetic vehicle* and this circulation may be *Self-regulated*, then we must assume that the *Self*, and its state of *Actualized Awareness*, directly relates to the ability to maintain optimum operation of the body via the *Will-Intention* of the *Alpha Spirit*.

Clear communication of this *Will-Intention* throughout *beta* ("physical") systems is directly **proportional** to the amount of personal defragmentation—because that is what determines the extent to which *Actualized Awareness* is *Self-directed*. Therefore, the whole ZU-line functions as a continuum un-

der the direction of *Self*. The more a *Seeker* can take responsibility for the experience and function of the universe they
are duplicating a communication of, the greater control
may be *directed*. As even expressed in the initial premise of
<u>Systemology: The Original Thesis</u>:—*"Responsibility equals Power."*

It is not difficult then to consider the "flow" of energy as an
analogy to the flow of air; its fragmentation, as a restriction
in flow. It is not necessary to devise an entire *yogic* tradition
of practiced breathing, assuming the *Seeker* is able to *Self-
direct* their own optimum regimens. There have been times
in the past when more the *Human Condition* experienced an
even greater amount of instruction and drilling in techniques than is applied today. We have since moved beyond
these paradigms into higher vistas, but that does not mean
that we should disregard former foundations of work that
have led us to this point.

Δ Δ Δ Δ Δ Δ Δ

Practice of breathing requires no instruction in Nature—nor
even to the individual that has not been severely *fragmented*
in their existence. But the modern *Human Condition*—the one
that is subjected to the constant societal bombardment of
energies and communications—is a different case altogether. The average individual does not take advantage of "full
breathing" and is often left at a personal disadvantage as a
result. The concept of the "full breath" (under various
names) is indicated among rudiments of virtually every
spiritual, mystical, esoteric or similar tradition of instruction. However, it is noticed that many *Seekers* employ these
practices only during a particular "meditation time" or
"ritual exercise" as opposed to permanently programming
the regular manner of everyday breathing.

For the *Seeker* that has not received such instruction from
former sources, the "full breath" is not a difficult activity to
learn, although at first some individuals may have to apply
more attention to the process before rhythms and methods

are a well practiced. Breathing methods are employed in most esoteric spiritual techniques, whether standing upright, seated or laying flat and straight on a comfortable carpet or bedding. Any position is acceptable so long as the extremities of the body are not constricted. The shoulders should be back and down, as should the diaphragm.

All breathing should also be conducted through the nose. And while there are a plethora of creative forms of "breath counting" or "rhythmic holds," these are primarily only effective exercises in earning greater control over the pace of breath and its full delivery throughout the *genetic vehicle*. Our experiments have not demonstrated that one set of "counts" or strained periods of retaining a breath have any greater results for our purposes. In fact, any rhythm that is labored or unnatural is not very practical. The delivery throughout the system as a "full breath" is more critical than the actual timing sequence that it is received.

There are various methods described throughout esoteric literature that pertain to energy work, visualization methods and the power of breath. The most appropriate order of circulation after intake is the abdomen area (diaphragm), then the middle of the chest, and finally the upper lungs. As such, the air is brought down to its deepest point and then elevated into the remainder of the chest and lungs. Although this is described here as a stepped-process, the *Seeker* is to practice making the full process a single action until it is a standard.

Breathing rhythm may be changed or managed by *Self-direction*; the automated pattern will shift according to the control center enforcing it. A person may regulate their breathing fully and consciously and thereby maintain full control over the composure of the physical body—or it may shift to a new patterned rhythm that coincides with some emotional reaction, especially as related to fragmentation—or fragmenting experience—that generally occur from day to day interaction and communication with the Physical

Universe (and other occupants of the same). It is curious that most individuals will only revert to their "natural breathing cycle" during sleep periods, when fragmentation is less consciously present in bio-mechanical activities of *genetic vehicles*. Describing this topic further would only unnecessarily complicate what is otherwise be a very clearly communicated message regarding the subject.

LECTURE EIGHT

. :: **BIOCHEMICAL FRAGMENTATION** :: .

IMPRINTS, DRUGS, TOXINS, RADIATION, PART- I

A basic introduction to *NexGen Systemology* sufficient enough for independent studies—at least as it pertains to the *Genetic Vehicle*—would not be complete without examining the nature of *physiological* and *biochemical* qualities regarding personal fragmentation; particularly concerning all communications of sensory experience and information concerning the *Physical Universe*. Keep in mind: so long as the *Alpha Spirit* is controlling a *genetic vehicle*, there is always a potential for (what we refer to as) "fragmentation" in *NexGen Systemology*—and this semantic of "fragmentation" is quite unique to our *Mardukite* paradigm.

Recent standards providing advancements of exploration into the subject of "fragmentation"—at lower *beta-levels* of personal experience—are explored quite fully in the "*Tablets of Destiny*" volume; then at slightly higher (more "intellectual") degrees of ZU-line activity within "*Crystal Clear*" textbook. Previously, however, I spent two decades exploring these concepts, which I now present so casually using *NexGen* semantics such as "**imprinting**" and "fragmentation." The premise behind these two specific aspects provided much of the original foundation for the paradigm of *NexGen Systemology* as a whole—and in spite of what is already written and presented within our current *NexGen* library (originally distributed exclusively by *Mardukite Truth Seeker Press* and now jointly managed by the *Joshua Free Publishing Imprint*), the concept is actually even far broader than is currently demonstrated at this *Grade*.

Case-in-point: I would like to consider a few facets in this chapter-lesson that may influence the nature of "imprints" and "fragmentation," which are otherwise not particularly treated in *Grade III* texts. I will provide a bit of background on this first, because all *Seekers* using our material—and certainly any dedicated *Systemologist*—should be quite familiar-ized with our concepts of *"imprinting"* and *"fragmentation."*

Whether we are treating a paradigm of semantics based in *Babylonian Star-Gates* or **Chakras** *of Eastern Mysticism*—or even some more modern methodology toward *Self-Actualization*—a *Seeker* is given demonstration that there is something "ar-tificial" attached to *Awareness* as *Self,* and some paradigms go as far as to suggest that these "artificial systems" are even *entities* or *identities* themselves, which are attached to the individual and their experience of existence. These "ar-tificial systems" imposed on the realization of the true and actual *Alpha Self* or *Alpha Spirit* are precisely what we treat as "fragmentation" in *Mardukite Systemology.*

So much prior (*Grade II*) material comprising the "*Mardukite Core*"—such as our "*Complete Anunnaki Bible*" and informa-tion contained in "*Sumerian Religon*" "*Babylonian Myth and Magic*" and "*Complete Book of Marduk by Nabu*"—is already dedicated toward defining "defragmentation" as it pertains to the ancient *Mardukite Babylonian Star-Gate* paradigm and semantics for a model of this progressive "ascent" or "**as-cension**" up a "ladder" or "*Pathway*" of, what we call, "*defragmentation*"—or else systematic reduction (or pro-cessed removal) of *fragmentation* from a system; in this case, systems that apply to-and-as *Self* and its *Identity-continuum.*

Concerning the modern legacy (the Mardukite paradigm) for our present purposes, the subject of *artificial fragmenta-tion* is introduced in the very first discourse of our *NexGen* field; and "*defragmentation*" is actually the title of the second discourse. Both of these discourses are still available for your view in our small reissued anthology—"*Systmology: The Original Thesis.*" All of these original discourses were quite quick reads; very pointedly written; similar to our recently released booklet *Mardukite Zuism: A Brief Introduction.* How-ever, I am still going to define these concepts here in this article (lecture), because a *Seeker* is immediately lost amidst semantics and *NewSpeak* in our paradigm without it. In fact, the clearest use of these terms and its premise is probably found in this original thesis of mine, where on one of the first few pages it states:—

> "The main key—insofar as the Human Condition has the ability to evolve beyond itself or what it's become —is not found in adoption of more 'Systems' or 'layers' of reasoning (and no additional external technologies are required to take this critical leap); rather it is found in the critical ability to systematically remove all the 'layers' of *Artificial Fragmentation* so all experiences, stimuli or data can be correctly— *Self-Honestly*—perceived and realized as existence and Reality."

Now, there are some *Seekers* that have not yet moved beyond their misunderstanding of these terms; and hence why it is so important to provide an introductory course that is both broad in its applications to higher points of "understanding" and *Awareness* achieved using *Mardukite Systemology*, but also completely relevant and applicable to the newcomer, in regards to, and demonstrable within, their everyday life as they are presently perceiving it.

To understand our methods and models, one must come to a realization that we are describing a "scale"—a "**gradient** scale"—when we refer to *Self-Honesty* and *Fragmentation*. They are, perhaps, best understood as two ends of an observable spectrum, similar to how we might consider "heat temperature." We can use a "thermometer" to effectively gauge the presence of "heat"—or more specifically "ambient heat"—in an area. There is an observable range on this meter and so, at the top of whatever parameter or fixed range we are using—because we know All extends to *Infinity* outside any range that we might plot—we can mark "*Self-Honesty*" at the top and "*Fragmentation*" at the bottom. You could just as easily distinguish other real qualities and mark, for example, the term "*Cause*" at the top and "*Effect*" at the bottom and then superimpose the *Standard Model* or

ZU-line over this. Such gradient scales are built into all demonstrations of existence and *Self*, using *NexGen Systemology* and the *Standard Model*.

> The *Seeker*—or rather their *Actualized ZU* as *Awareness* —is said to be in held in between some degree of "*Fragmentation*" and some degree of "*Self-Honesty*." This state of fluctuation is what provides the elements of "mystery" and "randomness" and "game" to the experience of *Reality*. Without such fragmented fluctuation, there is no "mystery" or "dark fields" present in our vision of *Awareness*.

For example, you take an optical lens, and you consider that the *True Self* or *Alpha Spirit* at its point of true existence (demonstrated at "7.0" on the *Standard Model Zu-Line*) is using this "scope" to look through the veils to receive communications from *beta-existence* using the *genetic vehicle*; and this perspective is only "true" and "clear" to the point or degree that the field and channel of communication "*de-fragmented*."

So, metaphorically: if we have a smudge on the lens, then that would be a "fragmentation"; or let us say we are flowing fluids through a pipe or channel that has some obstruction, then that would be a "fragmentation"; or when telephone land-lines used to have a lot of issues with dirty wires, connections and static and such; these would all be physical examples of "fragmentation" that disrupts clear communication of physical energy or power or whatever it may be that is transmitted or radiated. Anything of this nature is actually a systematic communication.

Just as I have given many examples of *fragmentation* as it applies to the physio-material universe, there are many many forms of personal *fragmentation* that may carry similarities and certain tendencies—certain patterns that we can even attribute various labels—but the exact nature of *fragmentation* is always specific or unique to the case of an individual.

What we call a "*Seeker*" in *Mardukite* and *NexGen Systemology* is an individual that is working their way through various processes and methods of personal *defragmentation* as a route to achieve, at the very least, the most basic state of *Self-Honesty* attainable in *beta-existence*. This is what the (*Grade III*) textbooks—"*Tablets of Destiny*" and "*Crystal Clear*" —are designed for; and what the intended purpose is behind (*Grade IV*) **"piloted"** assistance.

A basic state of Self-Honesty, once *actualized*—though certainly not the upper-most reach of spiritual ability within our paradigm—but this "basic state" is really what we are expecting as a minimum for our next evolution as *Homo Novus*. And we have discovered: this starts to have less to do with the biological organism directly and more to do with the WILL of the *Alpha Spirit* that is *Self-directed* along the ZU-line toward the control centers of the *genetic vehicle*. But this WILL as *Self-directed Intention* may only be effected to the degree that the channels are cleared of any fragmentary debris. All of these systems are interconnected on the continuum we refer to as the ZU-line; and any perceived "parts" of these things are just as systematically connected to relay of this information and energy as if there was only one mega-system in operation. Of course, we now know that there are actually multiple systems, working together, systematically, to comprise any conception one might ever have of *The System*—capital "T"; capital "S." Our best stab at such an understanding for this paradigm actually resulted in the *Standard Model* and *ZU-line*. Thus, it *is* possible to *know* real things in this lifetime; assuming of course you are grasping at something *real* to know about.

Δ Δ Δ Δ Δ Δ

Elsewhere in our *Grade III* materials, sufficient instruction is provided concerning this one type of *fragmentation* that we call "*Imprints*." For those who are not as familiarized yet with our semantic use of "*Imprinting*," it is defined within any *Version 3* "*NexGen Systemology Glossary*"—which you will find as an "appendix" in any *Grade III* volumes for *Mardukite Systemology*—and it reads:

> "To *Imprint* is to strongly impress, stamp, mark or outline onto a softer 'impressible' substance; or else to mark with pressure onto a surface or **slate**." (And, that's a very traditional definition of the word *Imprint*.) "In *NexGen Systemology*, the term *imprint* is used to indicate permanent Reality impressions marked by frequencies, energies or interactions experienced during emotional distress or antagonism to physical survival (such as unconsciousness or pain), all of which are stored with other reactive-response mechanisms at lower-levels of *Awareness* as opposed to the higher intellectual faculties of the 'Mind-System'; or an *imprint* may also be defined as an **experiential** 'memory-set' that may later **resurface** as Reality if triggered or restimulated artificially or by one's present environment, of which similar reaction-response systems engaged automatically in response based on an original *Imprint*."

It is not my goal to reiterate or condense several chapters worth of more advanced information into a few moments of this introductory article; suffice to say that we are dealing with a type of fragmentation called "emotional encoding" or else "imprinting." This is a different quality of fragmentation than the type that is generally "learned" or "programmed" by more traditional instructional or indoctrinate methods; hence we are not treating "intellectual ideas" in this case, but instead, the type of information that is retained specifically from "emotional imprinting," which we also call "encoding" when the imprinting sticks or holds in place. Therefore, we generally divide the quality of fragmentation into two primary categories: emotional encoding and intellectual programming.

Understand: we treat "emotional imprinting" as "encoded" and not "learned" in the conventional sense. Intellectual or mental programming relies on some other type of "logic" to support a communication relay and demonstration of information; whereas encoded imprinting relies on some type of "biochemical" or "emotional" quality for the information to receive substance. The "significance" is not based on intellectual facts, but on *sensation*. In any case, the actual associations of information may or may not be objectively valid or carry truth or be held in general agreement with the Physical Universe; but this *encoded imprinting* will be treated as true for the individual, by the individual themselves. This is really why this is important to know about.

If you want to have a good basic understanding of *Fragmentation* and *Self-Honesty* that is workable, it is simply easiest to treat them as opposites on a spectrum. You have got the idea of *fragmentation;* then you might understand *Self-Honesty* as the completely opposite state—or truest *"Alpha"* state—of clear "Knowingness" and *Self-directed* "Beingness" at the other end of this spectrum.

> The true ability of *Self* is never less
> than this perfected state,
> but *Actualized Awareness* may be dampened
> or diminished to a point where
> *Self* no longer has a clear and present
> handle on its own *Identity*.

This is very loosely along the same lines—in *beta-existence*—of when you hear someone use the expression that so-and-so "lost themselves" into something or another, but the truth is that nearly all *Alpha Spirits* operating a *genetic vehicle* for this *beta-existence* are doing so in some or another significant state of *fragmentation*—and of all the types, the information that we consider "imprinted" often poses the most significant energetic turbulence at low-level manifestations of experience. These imprints withhold the circulatory flow of *ZU-Awareness* below "2.0" on the Standard Model; which is also below the level of *Awareness* that we would consider "mental" functions.

The fact that *Imprinting* and *Emotional Encoding* is a *considera-tion* given significance "below" the *Awareness*-level of the "Mind-System" or intellect, is the very reason we treat the subject with a degree of importance in *NexGen Systemology*— because the *fragmentation* that takes place at this level can-not simply be "unlearned" in the manner of which "mental programming" might be "unlearned" using *right education*. That is, again, one of the issues regarding this type of *frag-mentation:* we are not dealing with learned information, because even erroneous facts, once accumulated, could be dissolved by simply choosing to "*un-learn*" or "*re-form*" or "*re-postulate*" former handling of intellectual facts.

Imprints may be treated in this manner at higher levels of *Self-Actualization*. Even if faulty and **fallacious** logic are en-twined in the programming, such higher level programming can be dissolved very easily with higher-level thought of similar magnitude. But, what about a *Seeker* while they are working up to these slightly higher-level realizations? How does a *Seeker* treat the lower-level *imprinting* that severely fragments and entwines our *Awareness* at the levels even be-low what we can readily observe as faulty logic? What about the contents of this thing we have called the "RCC"—*React-ive Control Center*—at "2.0" on the *Standard Model*?

Mental programming and intellectual or factual knowledge, even when it is wrong, is able to be treated at a higher range of intellectual faculties pertaining to a "*Mind-System.*" This information is also stored as a form of "mental imprint" or "**mental image**" that is quite complete and essentially holo-graphic in nature. It is stored as traditional memory like the film of a camera, and s most accessible for analytical recall. This would be equivalent to what a psychologist refers to as "salient memory" or "surface thought." This is, of course, not the only type of memory that is carried by an individu-al, but it stores the most accessible programming. The other type—"emotionally encoded imprinting"—reflects an en-tirely different type of information that actually supersedes higher abilities when viewed from the perspective of the physical body or *genetic vehicle*. We can easily say so, because when examining the ZU-line on the Standard Model, this "lower-level" *fragmentation* operates at frequencies that more closely match, share a higher **affinity** for, or simply are in closer proximity to, the direct physio-biochemical operations of the *genetic vehicle*.

Δ Δ Δ Δ Δ Δ

The two main aspects of *beta-fragmentation*—"emotional encoding" and "mental programming"—are interconnected concerning perceptual experience of *beta-existence*, but they are in many ways treated separately for *NexGen Systemology* studies and processing. We generally treat the subject of *emotional fragmentation* first—as described, for example, in "*Tablets of Destiny*"—before approaching any higher levels of *intellectual processing*—such as what a *Seeker* finds in "*Crystal Clear*." A *Seeker's* general state of fragmentation is thought to be a combination of both.

At the processing level of *Mardukite Systemology Grade III* and *IV*, we are primarily concerned with *encoding* and *programming* most readily accessible from *this* lifetime, although we certainly do no exclude the influence—or dare we say, "perturbation"—of past-life fragmentation, which is treated directly at even higher *Grades*. As should be clear at this juncture, the *Pathway to Self-Honesty* and *Gateways to Infinity* represent a progressive personal journey of increased *Awareness*; what we refer to as *Actualized Awareness*—that which is defragmented and completely under control of *Self* as *Alpha Spirit*; the true "*I-AM-Self.*"

This present series of introductory articles (lectures) has placed an emphasis on more tangible "work-a-day" world applications of *Mardukite* and *NexGen Systemology*. With that in mind: my intention is not to reiterate other readily available materials on the subjects of personal fragmentation, imprinting and defragmentation. In maintaining the spirit of this series, I would like to illustrate some very tangible elements found in personal fragmentation and defragment-ation that are not clearly relayed elsewhere—and which directly relate to the treatment of the *genetic vehicle* that has remained our primary focus here. Even if a *Seeker* has not yet studied this subject more deeply in our other materials and texts, it is easy to recognize that the *Human Condition* may be not only conventionally programmed at intellectual levels, but also encoded and imprinted upon using personal processes that very closely resemble what the psychologist calls "conditioning," although the clinical understanding of the same is not actually comparable to our own more widely encompassing holistic paradigm.

Presently we are concerned with aspects of *imprinting* and *fragmentation* directly linked to the physiological and bio-chemical systems of the living organism or *genetic vehicle*. What I mean is: we are now—at this stage—well aware of the nature of *imprints* and *programming*, the various methods by which memory is stored, *encoded* or even *learned*; however, we have also found that a considerable amount of this stored memory is erroneous, **implanted**, conditioned and often kept out of direct analytical view.

The *imprinting* I refer to all pertains directly with "associat-ive memory" that is probably the most subjective type of all possible **experiential-knowledge**. "Association Imprinting" forms as a result of *emotional encoding*; it operates well below the treatment of *Self-directed* "thought" and entwines en-ergy on the ZU-line, manifesting at degrees much closer to the lower frequency range of the physical organism or *ge-netic vehicle* itself. By this, I mean of course, *Imprinting* tied to emotional **neurotransmitters** and reactive biochemical processes that are "reactive" in nature, and generally plot-ted below "2.0" on the ZU-line.

Because this heavy fragmentation is "physiological," "emo-tional" and otherwise "biochemical" in nature, we find that it tends to respond very quickly to changes in physical en-vironment and other interactions between a *genetic vehicle* and the energies and matter that vibrate at similar frequencies. In brief: our personal experimentation suggests that significant amounts of *imprinting* and *encoded fragmentation* entwined at the "biochemical" range, is also held in place more strongly, kept hidden, or re-stimulated directly, by other interactions within the "biochemical range."

> For example: drugs, chemicals, toxins, food-additives, and other sources of "chemical fragmentation" may all actually render an individual—outside the state of *Self-Honesty*—far more susceptible to additional *imprinting*;
>
> –it affects stores or charge quality of *imprinting*;
>
> –it affects the ability to recognize the "RCC" *chains* and *sequences* directly related to *imprinting*; and
>
> –it certainly influences the *Awareness* necessary to reduce influences or entwined charges of personal ZU that are withheld from the individual's free use by the *Imprint*.

As you can see, this is certainly some pretty serious stuff that we have stepped into. This should provide something of a preview of what is in store for you as you take up this journey on the *Pathway to Self-Honesty* and beyond, to the *Gateways to Infinity*. But, of course, this journey has a specific starting point, and it starts *here*: making certain that we can maintain full control over the conditions of the physical body or *genetic vehicle* that is presently in use.

It should be well understood at this point that while we do very much set our sights on the highest vistas of *Self-Actualization* and a route toward the highest ideal states of the *Human Condition*, such ambitions once *realized*, may only be *actualized* by taking up the path of a workable methodology that will actually yield this result.

It requires a bit of work on your part.

The same methods used to *fragment* the *Human Condition*—the same systematic application of directed attentions, focus and conditioning—must all be processed out using a like energy and like force and focus. The way out, is the way through—at least if you want to go out the top. As such, we cannot dismiss the *fragmentation* taking place at lower frequencies pertaining to the biological level of the organism. We can select the choicest glass specimens for our telescopic view from *Self*, but if there is a smudge at the other end, then our intention of a clear view is obviously thwarted. Its important that we clean up that smudge; because all of the higher level applications of *defragmentation* seem rather ridiculous for us to shoot for with any certainty when the most basic, physical and identifiable sources of personal turbulence are left remaining unattended at the other end.

My intention here is not to **enforce** some personal moral opinion or ethic on lifestyle choice among the population. However, it remains quite obvious—to those of us looking, anyway—that there *is* a "Way"—or "Right Way"—which promotes a *rise* in personal *Actualized Awareness* and a total return to *Self* as the *Alpha Spirit*; and there are of course "ways" which do not promote such results, and which regardless of the tenacity and repeated effort applied, an individual is left with the task of fitting a square peg through a round hole, all of the while telling themselves they are dealing with octagons or something.

The Physical Universe is designed as such that it does require a little effort—a little work on our part—in order to make the *things "go"* and changes to manifest. And yet many individuals have succumb to a belief that the effort and thought, regardless of how it is applied, will somehow be "enough" to carry a clear intention forward; and of course, we know this is not the case.

We know that aside from human sentiment, this notion of "it's the thought that counts" or "well, you gave it your best effort" just doesn't seem to pan out in the actual Physical Universe.

We know that individuals caught up in their own "loops"—or "spun-in" on one or another avenue of approach—will just keep on attacking issues "their way" neurotically expecting some other result to take place; one that would actually defy causal or Cosmic Law if it were to take place.

Of course, the average fragmented individual does not know anything about this; they are expecting some miraculous magical break in the strongly enforced Reality agreements already put forth to carry the existence of this Physical Universe as we are experiencing it presently. (*I want to tackle this matter of the Physical Universe a bit more before we finish out this evening and our present lecture series—so, let's take a break first and meet back in fifteen.*)

LECTURE NINE

. :: **BIOCHEMICAL FRAGMENTATION** :: .

IMPRINTS, DRUGS, TOXINS, RADIATION, PART- II

To close this introductory series of articles, I would like to summarize with a concise treatment of the *Human Condition* in relationship to the present state of affairs on planet Earth. (*This is a continuation of the former chapter-lesson introducing "Biochemical Fragmentation."*) It is very important that a *Seeker* fully understands the nature of *"Imprinted Fragmentation"* when these words are used in *Mardukite* and *NexGen Systemology.* This is especially important before considering how strongly *Imprints* are affected by additional encounters, additional encoding and other facets of *biochemical fragmentation* including drugs, toxins, electronic interference and other types of radiation.

> Every individual occupying some attachment with the *Human Condition* has some kind of, or another, assorted *Imprinting* that is based on some type of emotionally encoded experience. This experience has a reactive-response component to it—such as the more primitive "fight-or-flight" reflex action—but actually, any basic behavior response-types may be encoded. The more strongly the emotional stimulation; the stronger the *Imprinting*.

Not all *Imprinting* is "unconscious" to us—but it does all contain highly charged emotional content. The more positive pleasurable moments in life do not seem to provide the same intense fragmentation even if they represent irrelevant data. It is mostly our perceived failures, shortcomings and pains of existence that provide us with the conditioned experience and encoding that results in the type of *Imprinting* we speak of at this Grade of *NexGen Systemology.*

For example: an individual might have a negative experience with some kind of "thing" or element in their youth and therefore form a conditioned response to this type of environmental stimulus in the future. This, in and of itself, is actually not any kind of new news regarding the *Human Condition*. However, what we have now discovered regarding *emotionally encoded imprints* is more than basic stimulus-response, as the psychologist might understand it.

> These holographic imprints are given personal significance as a result of personal emotion or emotional **investment** one has with the aspects, elements, or what we call "the facets" of an *Imprint*; and these can far exceed anything that is deemed "logical" or "analytical" concerning facets of an event or incident and its corresponding reactivity.

Whenever an *Imprint* is made, the total quality of the experience is **etched** onto a metaphoric slate or frame of film that we carry with us and which may be held up before our view at any time; either on command or by re-stimulation. Contents of any *Imprint* or memory may or may not be valid; but the stronger the emotion, the greater the impression made of the contents. And this impression encodes bits of data concerning all *facets* that are a part of the experience—almost like a snap-shot—including such information as time of day, weather, lighting, moisture in the air, and so forth; not to mention personal sensations, smells, tastes, skin pressures, physical actions; anything that contains some *facet* of the momentary *Imprinted* information.

Any *facet* may be "associated"—or "attached with a significance"—to whatever sensation or impression is received from the experience. All this encoded information is treated with the same emotional significance and association below the domain of "analytical thought"—and this is about as close to this thing that some call the "subconscious" that we are probably describing with our *Systemology*—because in *NexGen Systemology*, we actually acknowledge that a combination of all this information forms the literal content of an *Imprint*. (I would strongly suggest studying materials from

"*Tablets of Destiny*" for additional specifics regarding *Imprints* and emotional qualities of the Human Condition.

The purpose for introducing some of these more advanced *Systemology* concepts for our present "*Power of Zu*" article (lecture) series is:

Imprinting and *emotional encoding*
may take place *or* be re-stimulated into activity
at any time an individual experiences
a significant reduction of *Actualized Awareness.*

This same quality of fragmentation is even encouraged and reinforced chemically as a byproduct of many "agents" found in common everyday modern living. This is no small matter concerning the state of the *Human Condition*—and it is certainly no small matter when a *Seeker* has determined to take the route of *defragmentation.*

It should be understood that this true and faithful "ZU-knowledge" supersedes any moral imperative that undoubtedly may be attached to our "Right Way of Life" for religio-spiritual purposes and dogma, once an individual discovers it. But that is not our present purpose here; our purpose here lies strictly in what has been found effectively workable in actual practice. It should not be a real surprise that so many main tenets of our philosophy should concur with some or another older formerly known spiritual paradigms. This should only be viewed as a reflection of some unifying truth recognized about existence—which becomes easy to spot once it is recognized. Unfortunately, too many of these former models and methods seem to have fallen short of adequately communicating with the intensity and relevance necessary for present time.

You may find traces of this truth in ancient wisdom teachings, but the exact communication of the former messages do not seem to have been as widely heard throughout the world; certainly not to the same extent as intended by their originator. Or, when they have been heard, it seems as if the words have not been heard correctly.

The present state of the world is my only basis for this judgment and no other specific **demographic** or cultural bias is intended. Whether or not the full nature of the *Human Condition* is already understood by whatever unseen hand directs the systems governing human civilization, it should be clearly stated that the direction we have been guided toward, and the destination that humanity is headed on Earth, is precisely nowhere—or else, nowhere that will sustain the Prime Directive of our existence, which is: *To Exist*. Until such a time that you have *Self-Actualized* the *Alpha Spirit* to a point that you may choose to direct your *Self* to one or another physical alternative form at WILL—even a form that is not necessarily restricted to this planet—(until this time) there is every reason, even ethics aside, to preserve necessary conditions of physical life on Earth, with the utmost respect to the planet as a living organic system and the host of other lifeforms that it supports. The irresponsible enforcement of false power is what led the *Human Condition* toward conditions where it must make a very firm decision right now: to evolve or die.

A true spiritual evolution of the *Human Condition* is what is charted on the *Pathway to Self-Honesty*. Materials developed for *Grade III*—including "*Tablets of Destiny*" and "*Crystal Clear*" —provide a solid map that will extend the certainty and reach of the *Human Condition* far and beyond the state it has succumbed to. We also now have the much anticipated *Truth Seeker's Adventure Journal* available for those working through *Self-Processing* provided in the core textbooks.

These *Grade III* materials are not the "end-all" of everything we hope to aspire to—even within our still developing angle of approach—but *Grade III* is still literally milestones ahead of what has naturally taken place in the present human society happening around us today; meaning both **Western** and Eastern civilizations, for even the distant orient that once prided itself in its spiritual perfection aeons ago has since greatly detoured far from where it once was.

The entire planet Earth requires a healing and rehabilitation of spiritual ability—each and every living organism. It starts with the individual cell; the individual being; and this is where we have started: by strengthening *Actualized Awareness* and personal certainty of the individual.

Δ Δ Δ Δ Δ Δ

At this juncture we cannot be absolutely certain where the energy comprising *Imprints* and other personal *fragmentation* is actually stored on a physiological level. Since the emergence of a strong "New Thought" in early 20th century America, many ideas and theories have been put forth ranging from the "cellular level" to "DNA-genetics." It may very well be that the information is mainly stored at a more etheric astral level of existence and that this reel of film attached to our *Identity* is all that we are taking with us from this lifetime.

It may be that we actually take too much with us from this lifetime, and previous ones—all manner of *fragmentation* that still remains to be processed out. Of course, such subjects lead us into higher level *Systemological* pursuits—but for our present purposes, we can relay the idea of emotional encoding as interconnected to the physio-biochemical organism and its living systems in this lifetime and even the genetic memory it has stored from previous generations of cellular communication at a biological level. These systems —those which relate most closely to the *genetic vehicle*—are primarily chemical in nature.

When we discuss—as in previous articles for this series—the relationship of ZU to the food, water and air that is processed by the living organism, we are very specifically referring to chemical qualities of existence, substances, nutrients and means by which various chemicals are processed by organs composed of other chemicals. There is a certain chemical equilibrium that is sought to maintain optimum efficiency, though we know that the living organism is an "open system" and that with the constant reception and expulsion of chemicals, this is actually a continuous ongoing systematic process that is mainly following its own level of the Prime Directive: to maintain existence. There is an ongoing relationship between the *genetic vehicle* following its own encoding for existence and the *direction* and *determination* of the governing *Alpha Spirit*, which independently seeks its own optimum means of infinite survival.

There are several hindrances to upholding the Prime Directive ("to exist"), and the first one would obviously be negligence; another would be incidental injury; and then, of course, there is the physical entropy that seeks to enforce Cosmic Law of material deterioration of optimum conditions as a defining quality of physical "*time.*" These are the common ways in which most individuals "go out" from this world. Very few individuals actually "Ascend." The condition of "Ascension" is not guaranteed by a body-death. Yes, sure: after this incarnation, you would most certainly "leave behind" physical restrictions of your associative-identity with the most recently governed body; but that is no guarantee you will automatically access high levels of clear *Self-Actualization.*

Spiritual experiments for *Systemology* currently being conducted demonstrate most apparently that *Imprinting*—and most solidified types of personal fragmentation—are actually more permanent than we originally suspected; even carrying over from one experience of a lifetime to the next and continuing to affect the "**capability**"—or "capacity for the ability" to direct total *Self-Determined Awareness.*

If the highest ideals of "Ascension" were an automatic guarantee—if this were actually the case—there would be no systematic or functional purpose behind repeated lifetimes spent toward achieving this same result; since we can also ascertain that this same lofty goal is applied to an individual's spiritual "Great Work" for every current physical incarnation.

> We cannot even be certain, without a doubt, that the entire experience of the *Human Condition* is not, in itself, an incredibly powerful electronic *Imprint* that has been implanted and enforced on the *Alpha Spirit* for this beta-experience of Reality.

Many of these additional philosophic matters are generally taken up at higher *Grades* of knowledge because they do not, change more immediate tasks at hand for a *Seeker* to necessarily achieve their initial sure footing to start unfolding a personal journey on the *Pathway to Self-Honesty*.

It is quite simply in the greatest interest of the individual—the *Seeker*—and of benefit to all those they interact with as a *Reality Experience* in the Physical Universe, to attain (and maintain) the highest ideal state for the *Human Condition* possible during this lifetime. It is no exaggeration that the course taken—the *fate*—of the entire successive evolution of the *Human Condition* may very well rely on what you are doing right here and right now and what you are able to manifest for the future. Systemology provides you with the effective power of ten-million butterfly sneezes. There are very few things that can hinder the incredible potential waiting to unfold for a *Seeker*; but *fragmentation* is certainly one of them—and too often it goes unchecked while sights are set on some higher plane.

The natural biochemical organic processes of the *genetic vehicle*—which maintain its optimum function and health, coinciding with the clearest circulation of ZU energy—may be easily upset by many different sources of personal turbulence; most of which are simply taken for granted by individuals that have grown accustomed to the "modern way" of things without raising them to a scrutiny. There are many substances that can affect the processing and chemical equilibrium of the *genetic vehicle* inherent in the "modern way" of life: chemicals (natural and synthetic); drugs (again, natural or synthetic); dietary supplements (food additives and preservatives); toxins (pesticides, industrial chemicals, solvents and waste products); radiation (atomic, electromagnetic and even emotional); and every other application of external mechanical technologies—from automobiles, to X-ray machines, to atomic fission and nuclear bombs. There is no shortage of avenues leading toward—or directly reinforcing—one type or another of personal *fragmentation*; yet until relatively recently, there have been only shortages in surefire ways to properly manage and alter this convoluted universe composed of agreements so arcane and archaic that we can hardly even trace their origins; we simply adopt them and enforce our children to also agree.

Many aspects of "modern" living are taken for granted; once postulated and set in motion by someone in the long distant past and then left to run, or fed continuously to keep running, simply to maintain its place of holding up a delicate house-of-cards that represents the governing systems of the *Human Condition*. Any aspect of "modern" living contributory to *fragmentation*, including *chemical fragmentation*—meaning it affects *Self-determined* physio-biochemical functions of the *genetic vehicle*—should be taken into account as a *Seeker* personally journeys toward *Self-Honesty*. It is the same basic *Pathway* for all of us, but each individual will find their own unique *facets* of poorly associated knowledge to work out—or "**process out**"—during this lifetime on their ascent. Such *defragmentation* is a necessary condition of the ascent.

Poorly associated information often leads to setting up automated reactive-responses to the Physical Universe in the absence of true knowledge. The systematic reduction and elimination of this erroneous *encoding* is what defines *defragmentation* and a "way out" from trappings and limitations, which we have all at one time or another agreed to; and with each of these agreements, agreed to a reduced condition of personal *Self-determinism*. Repair of *Self-Determinism* is quite possible using the proper *processing* and rehabilitation of the control by the *Self* as *Alpha Spirit*; but a *Seeker* should be very certain that they are not working against themselves—and their true efforts toward achieving these goals—by continuing behavioral tendencies or contact with counter-productive counter-efforts that may hinder—or even render useless and null—the potential gains and wins of our various methods.

Δ Δ Δ Δ Δ Δ Δ

When you line up all of the truly effective "spirito-mystica-metaphysical" procedures that appear throughout the last 6,000 years of recorded history—and there are not very many effective and workable methods of note—each one carries and shares a particular commonality of practices or regimens with one another, which may be simply reduced to the most fundamental concept: PURIFICATION.

Regardless of which spiritual source from our past we might turn to for inspiration in, for example, developing the modern *NexGen Systemology* paradigm, we were **confronted** by one version or another of "*self-purification*" rites and formulas. These demonstrations are as commonly shared—across the boards—as the theme of INITIATION, which is defined at the end of "*Crystal Clear*." But mystic rites and esoteric rules of *purification* actually precede the steps of *Initiation*.

An "Initiate" is always to present themselves for "initiation ceremonies" only after a period dedicated to personal *purification*. Of course, in *NexGen Systemology*, we treat the truth of this without necessarily participating or conjuring up one or another brand of "traditional esoterica"—such as might be explored more thoroughly within its own playing field (in *Grade I*), where I previously provided necessary instruction throughout such volumes as: "*Sorcerer's Handbook*" and "*The Druid's Handbook*" and "*Elvenomicon*" and "*The Great Magickal Arcanum*" and so forth.

By comparison, work of *Grade III* in no way contradicts these former paradigms; but in *Mardukite* and *NexGen Systemology*, we treat a unification of former understandings at a higher order of reasoning—and with an appropriate semantic paradigm that is not restricted to one or another of these former paradigms. Our goal—my goal—in developing *Systemology* was (*and is*) the highest echelon of understanding possible outside of any paradigm; and should any of this somehow directly **validate** something else from back down the timeline, well... *great!* But, understand that this is not in any way what my direct intention is regarding this new *NexGen* understanding of the universe.

Whether using some version of obscure medieval sorcery out of an old archaic dusty grimoire, or perhaps attempting to contact your *Self* in some round-about convoluted way as described by wizards like Abramelin; whom after six months of "pious living" and purification treatments would then make contact with *Self* as some external identity commonly referred to as the "Holy Guardian Angel" in some ceremonial magic traditions, or the "Higher Genius" and so forth—they have a lot of names for this thing called *Self*— and perhaps this premise is even set forth with an ancient foreknowledge that there are multiple "entities" interacting, or influencing, what is experienced as the Identity as-for-and-by *Self*. But, the point to keep in mind here is: even this arcane experimental sorcerer type still carefully observed purification periods before even bothering to apply ritualized efforts to explore new vistas—or open up new gateways of understanding.

Checks and balances at work in the universe. The more clearly observant and *Aware* the *Seeker* is about these basic Laws governing the Cosmos—referred to on the arcane tablets as "*cosmic ordering*" as the *Awareness* of *Self* observes the moves and turns taking place in *this* realization of the Physical Universe—the more "amazing" or "magical" the individual appears to be for those who have not yet attained this same level of *Actualized Awareness*; because they are radiate an understanding and certainty of a higher order of reason. Even though they may share proximity—in a similar physical space—with another individual, they are operating an understanding in all of their activities in a way that is far and above the baseline standard issue programmed one-foot-in-front-of-the-other robotic method that most people have simply become accustomed to getting through their daily existence with; and by succumbing to the perceived least-effort comfort-ability of that, they proceed to arrange robotic determinism of one-foot-in-front-of-the-other right into a grave without *knowing* anything substantial that may be useful for arranging the next level of *beingness*.

When one examines the regimens of monks and shamans: we find equal significance given to the health and strength of the physical body or *genetic vehicle*—and its *purification*—as we find given to treatments of the spiritual and astral levels of existence, which compose the more colorful esoteric and mystical lore that survives in the "New Age" today. To *detoxify,* they suggest a regimen of light exercise (walking or jogging) to increase circulatory flow followed by the use of a "sweatlodge" or *sauna* to literally purge the body of its *chemical fragmentation*. Fluids, minerals and vitamin-nutrients are also supplemented to regulate and stabilize personal chemistry of the *genetic vehicle* during the process.

Many individuals—when left unaided—often do not change "their ways" because of the sensation of "withdrawal" that often occurs. And many modern practitioners and spiritualists and "New Agers" of every flavor, have too often overlooked the benefits gained from "pious lifestyles" maintained by those we have admired in the past, which have tread this *Pathway* before us, that have achieved—or at least demonstrated some degree of achievement—of true Ascension.

Too often, this idea of fluffing—"positive thinking" or "creative visualization" or a few minutes spent in front of the mirror chanting "axioms" or "affirmations"—is not enough to override lifetimes of bombardment—or even the interference **prevalent** in a single lifetime in the "modern" world. The *Human Condition* requires a bit more assistance now to grant the certainty necessary to rise up and **confront** the sources of turbulence—thereby preventing further (additional) fragmentation.

The primitive magics of any era have only partially resolved the problems by providing a momentary glimpse of something more—something greater than—but too often the individual gets to "thinking" again and snaps their *Awareness* right back to where they were. My goal is to provide a solid route of certainty that will permit any individual living today or tomorrow—or whenever they show up in their cells here—the means, tackle and gear to make their way back out; through and out. What we have actually accomplished with *Grade III* is not necessarily the final leg of the journey that goes all the way out, but our research has demonstrated that those working successfully within this *Grade* are, at the very least, not getting any worse; and they are seeing real progress forward. And as they are able to radiate a more vibrant personal ZU frequency into their physical existence, it is becoming noticeable to those around them that something has changed—and they find out that they are more able to handle and manage the confusions and fragmentation of the world because their attention is fixed on a very real point with certainty—a greater certainty than what they worldly domains have to offer; and that point is nowhere confined to this Physical Universe.

We have discovered that the more an individual is persuaded to concern ourselves with the turbulent confusion of the world-at-large head on—outside of a state of *Self-Honesty* —the more likely they are to be wrapped up in it; to be *of* it, and not just play at the games *within* it. This is when an individual is likely to lose their own *Self-determinism* and participate with a series of agreements that keep shifting the postulates around to base our *Reality*, concerning, for example, what does or does not make us sick; then on the other side, what makes us well and sane. We are asked to flip-flop our beliefs regarding the medicines and poisons of life—and I can assure you that rather than take the stand of advisement in contrary to some FDA or other health regulation, I can tell you that these suggestions and minimums and supposed regulations are not severe enough.

Existing regulations presently in place now mainly serve business interests and perhaps provide only a marginal modicum of environmental damage control; because of course, if things were on a decline too obviously, then certainly someone would notice—someone would notice and take the responsibility to change things. We would expect. We would hope. Ah, but *hope* is one of the last points before *Awareness* drops out and we are no longer cause; because when we are lingering around in *hope*, we are waiting as an effect—the responsibility now displaced elsewhere.

Interestingly, we have known certain things for a long time —certain things about our planet and about our activities— and again, we are not about to make a specific appeal to your political side with our philosophy. There is no political matter involved here. It is a matter of *Life* and *Livingness.* It does not matter what side you take on a political regard, because we know the dramatics and entertainment behind social politics is just another fabrication of someone's **imagination** that has been left to run on its own now—the responsibility for that long passed into the shadows when there was actually a "Divine Right to Rule" in place.

The real agenda is hardly covert, hidden or a conspiracy; when one can determine it quite clearly with a *Self-Honest* examination of what is happening around us every day. It is worthless if I am to stand here and point the things all out to you. That's not interesting to me and it feels too much like indoctrination for you. Therefore, it is abundantly clear to me that we can best apply efforts toward increase of ability for the *Human Condition* to operate in *Self-Honesty* and see things as they really are without the installation of dogma; which is a far more important loftier goal than me just telling you how things really are.

Unveiling this personal mystery is something a *Seeker* discovers when using *processing* techniques of *Systemology*. There are many exercises and procedures that we conduct that do not seem to have any real value to them until a person actually *does* come to those *realizations* for themselves in the process. There is far greater value in receiving truth via these **gnostic** channels of pure cognition as opposed to my kicking this spiritual movement off with a large book of dry academic postulates and lists of facts about how things are in the universes. *Systemology* is, and will always be, a route of *Self-knowledge*, which can only be determined as true to the extent that is found effective by *Self*.

The final subject I wish to touch upon for this series concerns a return to a world problem that has plagued us since the end of the second World War—and yet too often now is either misunderstood or ignored entirely. RADIATION. We are literally surrounded by it everyday. There is even a background radiation present, back of the entire Physical Universe, which is unavoidable to contact so long as an organism is present *in* the Physical Universe. But cosmic radiation is only one source of potential "chemical fragmentation" and a minor one at best, since we now have come to discover many greater sources of harmful radiations; either by unearthing them or generating them as byproducts of our industrialization.

Authorities have always each gone in their own directions—often inspired by their own political, business and financial-power agendas—concerning any official opinions regarding effects on the *Human Condition*—or even the linger effects of their original and ongoing nuclear tinkering altogether; but this displacement of responsibility only ensures that these problems are certain to be with us for a very long time. The fact is that we are again returning to an era of testing and

standoffs regarding the weaponized use of devices that directly **conflict** with the utilitarian ethics of our *Systemology.**
It is likely that this is going to have a visible effect on the
health of the public condition—including the general state
of morale concerning a continuing existence into the future.
So long as the *Human Condition* is held suspended in present
problems reacted to by past programming, there is little
hope for charting an appropriate future to support the most
ideal conditions for *Life* to exist; and to be certain that it
may continue to go on existing for many generations to
come.

On a higher level of understanding, the issues of *nuclear* and
electromagnetic "radiation" and other cumulative *toxins* and
chemical sources of fragmentation all contribute toward a
reduction in health and *Awareness* for the *Human Condition.*
Contact with and absorption of many components found in
our "modern" world are "contagions" for illness for those
who are consistently exposed or chronically maintain lower
ZU frequencies. One reason is that all forms of *fragmentation*
are cumulative in effect—stored and carried over the entire
lifetime of an individual, with many aspects even carried
over into multiple lifetimes.

As a holistic approach to understanding and managing the
fundamentals of the *Human Condition*, there are factors to
consider that extend even beyond physical nature of radiation itself. There is the general condition of "mental
health" and "spiritual wellbeing" to consider, regarding a
population held in emotional paralysis by one source or another, promoting everything from general worry to blatant
hysteria. All these states and conditions serve only to reinforce positions of uncertainty for the individual—especially
when we are said to be a part of a group, a society, a nation
or a race and we haven't the foggiest clue of why things are
going on in our name. This also successfully fragments the
individual, the group, the society, nation and race—all at
once.

---

* See *"Mardukite Zuism—Brief Introduction"* given previously.

And this is what we are here to learn to resolve; this is what the fundamentals of *Systemology* reveal when applied to the world around us. We are starting with the individual and bringing them to an increased capacity for ability that will lead us to a true continued existence that is *Self-Honest* and true; not just true for one—but true for all. And this level of truth *is* very much attainable in this existence—during this lifetime—no matter what anyone has said to you.

> You can *know*. You can *do*.
> And you can *be*.

And I believe we are off to the right start if anything that I have said in these preliminary articles (lectures) has been found effective for you, or inspiring to you, in generating the momentum of that first step forward in this direction.

There are many more aspects to *Mardukite Zuism* and *NexGen Systemology*—many new vistas and discoveries that can be shared with you; but for now, I would like to leave you with these kernels that have been put forth, in hopes that these few small seeds will germinate into something real that you can grasp, so that when you come back looking to know the rest, you will not have to know it on *faith* and *trust*; you will be able to recognize that it is true and real, because you will *know* that it is true and real.

You will know for yourself, because you know yourself. I am simply here holding a door open for you.

So just mind the gap and pass through.

You have friends waiting to welcome you on the other side.

appendix

+ The Creed of Mardukite Zuism +
+ Marduk's Tablet of Destiny +
+ The Anunnaki Tablet of Union +
+ Systemology Glossary +
+ Suggested Reading +

THE CREED OF MARDUKITE ZUISM.
PRINCIPLES OF BELIEF.*

1.) We believe in an Absolute Being, which is Infinite —(the ABZU)—the All-as-One encompassing Source of all Being, Knowing and Awareness to all Alpha/Spiritual (AN) and Beta/Physical (KI) states of existence.

2.) We believe in a spiritual energy of all Life and Awareness (ZU) in the physical universe that is an effect of a spiritual cause; a Spirit that is cause. This Spirit—in its Alpha state—is the True Self "I-AM" Individual Identity that many have called the "soul."

3.) We believe that the Human Condition is a genetic vehicle used by a spiritual source (AN) to experience the Finite as physical existence (KI)—that we are Awareness (ZU) projected onto a genetic vehicle—and that while the vehicle/body may perish to physical entropy, the "Alpha Spirit" remains immortal and Self-directed to the extent of its own Actualized Awareness.

4.) We believe that the highest form of worship and spirituality is the actualization and advancement of our "Self" as Spirit in Self-Honesty—and that Self-Honesty is the I-AM Alpha state of Being and Knowing, which is realizable in this lifetime.

5.) We believe that the purpose of all existence is: to exist—and that the prime directive of all spiritual Life is: continued existence of spiritual Life and co-creation of habitable Reality. "Good" and "Moral" actions are evaluated to the extent of this end.

6A.) We believe that no Life exists in exclusion to all other Life—and that the conditions of a habitable

---

* First drafted in 2019 by Joshua Free with Kyra Kaos.

Reality extending from Self include: Home; Community; All Humanity; All Life on Earth; All Life in the Universe; All Spiritual Life; and the Infinite.

6B.) We believe in a continued evolution of Alpha Spirit awareness developed beyond one physical life, and that a Spirit experiences many.

7A.) We believe Mardukite Zuism is: a 21st Century AD synthesis of the 21st Century BC wisdom collected on cuneiform tablets and experienced in ancient Mesopotamia, esp. Babylon.

7B.) This cuneiform library includes details concerning: beings called the Anunnaki; ordering of the Cosmos; creation of Humanity; and an entire legacy of systematized traditions.

8.) We believe in the continuation of, and proper communication of, the legacy of true Human history —and the ability of every Human to realize that they are a Free Spirit in a Free Zone of Self-Determinism: No "evils" can affect intentions if an individual is spiritually Self-Actualized in Self-Honesty.

THE ARCANE KNOWLEDGE FROM MARDUK'S TABLET OF DESTINY.*

1.) As above, so below; On earth as it is in Heaven
   an-bala ki-bala an-ba ki an-ba

2.) What the Mind believes, the Spirit reinforces
   da-ga nam-ku-zu dingir-Lamma a bi-ib-gar

3.) When disaster is self-made, no man can interfere
   nig-ku-lam-ma dingir-ra-na-ka su—tu-tu nu-ub-zu

4.) What is given in submission is a catalyst for defiance
   nig-gu-gar-ra nig-gaba-gar-ra

5.) Whoever partners with Truth, creates Life
   nig-ge-na-ta a-ba in-da-di nam-ti i-u-tu

---

*   Excerpted from *"The Tablets of Destiny"* by Joshua Free.

THE ARCANE KNOWLEDGE FROM THE ANUNNAKI TABLET OF UNION.*

All Life is precious for the fact that it lives.
Life *IS* – existing against all odds,
And Life grows and develops following a course.
Love is Will – and Love creates Emotion.
Love is everything in this world.
God is the Supreme Being,
That which represents True Pure All-Powerful Love,
The Light that binds and unites the Universe
In its Creation and Destruction.

God is the conscience at the center of all Life.
When you put Love and Light into Life, which is God,
The Spirit of that Life is Eternal.
The "Devil" is a name given to the path that leads
To harming one another and the Self
Against the Natural Order,
And promoting the belief that one can live without Love.
You cannot exist without Love.

Love is even in what is considered "Evil," for it to exist.
As the Love in "Evil" manifests the Demons of Jealousy,
Demons of Misery, Greed, Pain and Grief.

The Power to Create is in Love
And the Power to Destroy is in Love.
To live for yourself alone outside of Love
Is union with Greed.

As the Love of God is in all Life,
The Natural State of Unity in all Life
IS to Love all Life.

---

* Excerpted from *Mardukite Tablet-R (2009)*; reprinted in "*The Complete Anunnaki Bible*" edited by Joshua Free.

NEXGEN SYSTEMOLOGY GLOSSARY.*

A-for-A (one-to-one) : an expression meaning that what we say, write, represent, think or symbolize is a direct and perfect reflection or duplication of the actual aspect or thing—that "A" is for, means and is equivalent to "A" and not "a" or "q" or "!"; in the relay of communication, the message or particle is sent and perfectly duplicate in form and meaning when received.

acknowledgment : a response-communication establishing that an immediately former communication was properly received, duplicated and understood; the formal acceptance and/or recognition of a communication or presence.

activating event : an incident or occurrence that automatically stimulates a conscious or unrecognized reminder or 'ping' from an earlier *imprinting incident* recorded on one's own personal timeline as an emotionally charged and encoded memory; an incident or instance when thought systems are activated to determine the consequence or significance of an activity, motion or event—often demonstrated as *Activating Event → Belief Systems → Consideration.*

actualization : to make actual, not just potential; to bring into full solid Reality; to realize fully in *Awareness* as a "thing."

affinity : the apparent and energetic *relationship* between substances or bodies; the degree of *attraction* or repulsion between things based on natural forces; the *similitude* of frequencies or waveforms; the degree of *interconnection* between systems.

agreement (reality) : unanimity of opinion of what is "thought" to be known; an accepted arrangement of how things are; things we consider as "real" or as an "is" of "reality"; a consensus of what is real as made by standard-issue (common) participants; what an individual contributes to or

---

*   Excerpted from *NexGen Systemology Dictionary v.4.4*; only those words which actually appear in this present volume are included.

accepts as "real"; in *NexGen Systemology*, a synonym for "*reality.*"

allegorical : a representation of the abstract, metaphysical or "spiritual" using physical or concrete forms.

alpha : the first, primary, basic, superior or beginning of some form; in *NexGen Systemology*, referring to the state of existence operating on spiritual archetypes and postulates, will and intention "exterior" to the low-level condensation and solidarity of energy and matter as the 'physical universe'.

alpha-spirit : a "spiritual" *Life*-form; the "true" *Self* or I-AM; the *individual*; the spiritual (*alpha*) *Self* that is animating the (*beta*) physical body or "*genetic vehicle*" using a continuous *Lifeline* of spiritual ("*ZU*") energy; an individual spiritual (*alpha*) entity possessing no physical mass or measurable waveform (motion) in the Physical Universe as itself, so it animates the (*beta*) physical body or "*genetic vehicle*" as a catalyst to experience *Self*-determined causality in effect within the *Physical Universe*; a singular unit or point of *Spiritual Awareness* that is *Aware* that it is *Aware.*

alpha thought : the highest spiritual *Self-determination* over creation and existence exercised by an Alpha-Spirit; the Alpha range of pure *Creative Ability* based on direct postulates and considerations of *Beingness*; spiritual qualities comparable to "thought" but originating in Alpha-existence (at "6.0") independently superior to a *beta-anchored* Mind-System, although an Alpha-Spirit may use Will ("5.0") to carry the intentions of a postulate or consideration ("6.0") to the Master Control Center ("4.0").

amplitude : the quality of being *ample*; the size or amount of energy that is demonstrated in a *wave.* In the case of audio waves, we associate amplitude with "volume." It is not a statement about the frequencies of waves, only how "loud" they are—to what extent they are or may be projected (or audible).

AN : an ancient "Sumerian" cuneiform sign for Heaven or "God"; in *Mardukite Zuism and Systemology* designating the *'spiritual zone'* (or *'Alpha Existence'*); the *Spiritual Universe*

—comprised of spiritual matter and spiritual energy; a direction of motion toward spiritual *Infinity*, away from or superior to the physical (*'KI'*); the spiritual condition of existence providing for our primary *Alpha* state as an individual *Identity* or *I-AM-Self* which interacts and experiences *Awareness* of a *beta* state in the *Physical Universe* (*'KI'*) as *Life*.

anchor (conceptual) : a stable point in space; a fixed point used to hold or stabilize a spatial existence of other points; a spatial point that fixes the parameters of dimensional orientation, such as the corner-points of a solid object in relation to other points in space; in *NexGen Systemology*, "beta-anchored" is an expression used to describe the fixed orientation of a viewpoint from Self in relation to all possible spatial points in *beta-existence* ("physical universe"), or else the existential points that fix the operation of the "body" within the space-time of *beta-existence*.

Ancient Mystery School : the original arcane source of all esoteric knowledge on Earth, concentrated between the Middle East and modern-day Turkey and Transylvania c. 6000 B.C. and then dispersing south (Mesopotamia), west (Europe) and east (Asia) from that location.

apparent : visibly exposed to sight; evident rather than actual, as presumed by Observation; readily perceived, especially by the senses.

a-priori : from "cause" to "effect"; from a general application to a particular instance; existing in the mind prior to, and independent of experience or observation; validity based on consideration and deduction rather than experience.

archetype : a "first form" or ideal conceptual model of some aspect; the ultimate prototype of a form on which all other conceptions are based.

ascension : actualized *Awareness* elevated to the point of true "spiritual existence" exterior to *beta existence*. An "Ascended Master" is one who has returned to an incarnation on Earth as an inherently *Enlightened One*, demonstrable in their actions —they have the ability to *Self-direct* the "Spirit" as *Self*, just as we are treating the "Mind" and "Body" at this current grade of instruction; previously treated in *Moroii ad Vitam* as a state of Beingness after *First Death*, experienced by an *etheric body*, which is able to maintain consciousness as a personal identity continuum with the same *Self-directed* control and communication of Will-Intention that is exercised, actualized and developed deliberately during one's present incarnation.

associative knowledge : significance or meaning of a facet or aspect assigned to (or considered to have) a direct relationship with another facet; to connect or relate ideas or facets of existence with one another; a reactive-response image, emotion or conception that is suggested by (or directly accompanies) something other than itself; in traditional systems logic, an equivalency of significance or meaning between facets or sets that are grouped together, such as in $(a + b) + c = a + (b + c)$; in NexGen Systemology, erroneous associative knowledge is assignment of the same value to all facets or parts considered as related (even when they are not actually so), such as in $a = a$, $b = a$, $c = a$ and so forth without distinction.

assumption : the act of taking or gather to one's Self; taking possession of.

attention : active use of *Awareness* toward a specific aspect or thing; the act of "attending" with the presence of *Self*; a direction of focus or concentration of *Awareness* along a particular channel or conduit or toward a particular terminal node or communication termination point; the Self-directed concentration of personal energy as a combination of observation, thought-waves and consideration; focused application of *Self-Directed Awareness*.

authoritarian : knowledge as truth, boundaries and freedoms dictated to an individual by a perceived, regulated or enforced "authority."

awareness : the highest sense of-and-as Self in knowing and being as I-AM (the *Alpha-Spirit*); the extent of beingness directed as a POV experienced by Self as knowingness.

Babylonian : the ancient Mesopotamian civilization that evolved from *Sumer*; inception point for systematization of civic society and religion.

band : a division or group; in *NexGen Systemology*, a division or set of frequencies on the ZU-line that are tuned closely together and referred to as a group.

beta (awareness) : all consciousness activity ("*Awareness*") in the "Physical Universe" (KI) or else *beta-existence*; *Awareness* within the range of the *genetic-body*, including material thoughts, emotional responses and physical motors; personal *Awareness* of physical energy and physical matter moving through physical space and experienced as "time"; the *Awareness* held by *Self* that is restricted to a physical organic *Lifeform* or "*genetic vehicle*" in which it experiences causality in the *Physical Universe*.

beta (existence) : all manifestation in the "Physical Universe" (KI); the "Physical" state of existence consisting of vibrations of physical energy and physical matter moving through physical space and experienced as "time"; the conditions of *Awareness* for the *Alpha-spirit* (*Self*) as a physical organic *Lifeform* or "*genetic vehicle*" in which it experiences causality in the *Physical Universe*.

beta-defragmentation : toward a state of *Self-Honesty* in regards to handling experience of the "Physical Universe" (*beta-existence*); an applied spiritual philosophy (or technology) of Self-Actualization originally described in the text "*Crystal Clear*" (*Liber-2B*), building upon theories from "*Systemology: The Original Thesis*."

biological unconsciousness : the organism independent of the sentient *Awareness* of the *Self* to direct it; states induced by severe injury and anesthesia.

capable : the actual capacity for potential ability.

catalyst : something that causes action between two systems or aspects, but which itself is unaffected as a variable of this energy communication; a medium or intermediary channel.

chakra : an archaic Sanskrit term for "wheel" or "spinning circle" used in *Eastern* wisdom traditions, spiritual systems and mysticism; a concept retained in NexGen Systemology to indicate etheric concentrations of energy into wheel-mechanisms that process *ZU* energy at specific frequencies along the *ZU-line*, of which the *Human Condition* is reportedly attached *seven* at various degrees as connected to the Gate symbolism.

channel : a specific stream, course, current, direction or route; to form or cut a groove or ridge or otherwise guide along a specific course; a direct path; an artificial aqueduct created to connect two water bodies or water or make travel possible.

charge : to fill or furnish with a quality; to supply with energy; to lay a command upon; in *NexGen Systemology*—to imbue with intention; to overspread with emotion; application of *Self-directed (WILL)* "intention" toward an emotional manifestation in beta-existence; personal energy stores and significances entwined as fragmentation in mental images, reactive-response encoding and intellectual (and/or) programmed beliefs; in traditional mysticism, to intentionally fix an energetic resonance to meet some degree, or to bring a specific concentration of energy that is transferred to a focal point, such as an object or space.

circuit : a circular path or loop; a closed-path within a system that allows a flow; a pattern or action or wave movement that follows a specific route or potential path only; in *NexGen Systemology*, "*communication processing*" pertaining to a specific flow of energy or information along a channel; *see* also "*feedback loop.*"

clockwork : rigidly fixed gear-like systems that operate mechanically and directly upon one another to function; a "clockwork universe theory" is a "closed-system design" popular in Newtonian Physics attributes all actions of energy-matter in space-time as reactions in accordance with a "Divine Decree" or fixed design that functions like a "clock-mechanism" and does not account for the "Observer."

codification : process of collecting, analyzing and then arranging knowledge in a standardized and more accessible systematic form, often by subject, theme or some other designation.

collapsing a wave : also, "*wave-function collapse*"; in *Quantum Physics*, the concept that an Observer is "collapsing" the wave-function to something "definite" by measuring it; defining or calculating a wave-function or inter-action of potential interactions by an Observation; in *NexGen Systemology*, when a wave of potentiality or possibility be-cause a finite fixed form; Consciousness or *Awareness* "collapses" a wave-function of energy-matter as a necessary "third" Principle of Apparent Manifestation (first described in *"Tablets of Destiny"*); potentiality as a wave is collapsed into an apparent *"is"*, the energy of which is freed up in systematic processing by *"flattening"* a "collapsed" wave back into its state of potentiality.

command : in *Metahuman Systemology*, responsibility and ability of Self (I-AM) as operating from its ideal "exterior" *Point-of-View* as Alpha Spirit; to direct communication for control of the *genetic vehicle* and Mind-Body connection that is perfectly duplicated from a source-point to a receipt-point along the ZU-line.

communication : successful transmission of information, data, energy (&tc.) along a message line, with a reception of feedback; an energetic flow of intention to cause an effect (or duplication) at a distance; the personal energy moved or acted upon by will or else 'selective directed attention'; the 'messen-ger action' used to transmit and receive energy across a medium; also relay of energy, a message or signal—or even locating a personal POV (viewpoint) for the Self—along the *ZU-line*.

condense (condensation) : the transition of vapor to liquid; denoting a change in state to a more substantial or solid condi-tion; leading to a more compact or solid form.

condition : an apparent or existing state; circumstances, situ-ations and variable dynamics affecting the order and function of a system; a series of interconnected requirements, barriers and allowances that must be met; in "contemporary language," bringing a thing toward a specific, desired or in-tentional new state (such as in "conditioning"), though to minimize confusion about the word "condition" in our literat-ure, *NexGen Systemology* treats "contemporary conditioning" concepts as imprinting, encoding and programming.

conflict : the opposition of two forces of similar magnitude along the same channel or competing for the same terminal; the inability to duplicate another POV; a thought, intention or communication that is met with an opposing counter-thought or counter-intention that generates an energetic cluster.

confront : to come around in front of; to be in the presence of; to stand in front of, or in the face of; to meet "face-to-face" or "face-up-to"; additionally, in *NexGen Systemology*, to fully tolerate or acceptably withstand an encounter with a particular manifestation or encounter.

consciousness : the energetic flow of *Awareness*; the Principle System of *Awareness* that is spiritual in nature, which demonstrates potential interaction with all degrees of the Physical Universe; the *Beingness* component of our existence in *Spirit*; the Principle System of *Awareness* as *Spirit* that directs action in the Mind-System.

consensual (consensus) : formed or existing simply by consent—by general or mutual agreement; permitted, approved or agreed upon by majority of opinion; knowingly agreed upon unanimously by all concerned; to be in agreement on the objective universe and/or a course of action therein.

consideration : careful analytical reflection of all aspects; deliberation; determining the significance of a "thing" in relation to similarity or dissimilarity to other "things"; evaluation of facts and importance of certain facts; thorough examination of all aspects related to, or important for, making a decision; the analysis of consequences and estimation of significance when making decisions; in *NexGen Systemology*, the postulate or Alpha-Thought that defines the state of beingness for what something "*is.*"

continuity : being a continuous whole; a complete whole or "total round of"; the balance of the equation ["–120" + "120" = "0" &tc.]; an apparent unbroken interconnected coherent whole; also, as applied to Universes in *NexGen Systemology*, the lowest base consideration of space-time or commonly shared level of energy-matter apparent in an existence, or else the lowest degree of solidity or condensation whereby all mass that exists is identifiable or communicable with all other mass that exists; represented as "0" on the *Standard Model* for the Physical Universe (*beta-existence*), a level of existence that is below Human emotion, comparable to the solidity of "rocks" and "walls" and "inert bodies."

continuum : a continuous enduring uninterrupted sequence or condition; observing all gradients on a *spectrum*; measuring quantitative variation with gradual transition on a spectrum without demonstrating discontinuity or separate parts.

control (systems) : Communication relayed from an operative center or organizational cluster, which incites new activity elsewhere in a system (or along the *ZU-line*).

correlate : a relationship between two or more aspects, parts or systems.

Cosmic Law : the "Law" of Nature (or the Physical Universe); the "Law" governing cosmic ordering; often called "Natural Law" in sciences and philosophies that attempt to codify or systematize it.

cosmology : a systematic philosophy defining origins and structure of an apparent Universe.

Cosmos : archaic term for the "Physical Universe"; semantically implies chaos brought into order; in *NexGen Systemology*, can also include considerations of "Universes" experienced previously as a *beta-existence*.

counter-productive : contrary to the greater or original purpose or intention; in *NexGen Systemology*, anything which brings *Life* away from its sustainable goal or position of *Infinite Existence*.

Crystal Clear : the second professional publication of Mardukite Systemology, released publicly in December 2019; the second professional text in Grade-III Mardukite Systemology, released as "*Liber-2B*" and reissued in the Grade-III Master Edition "*Systemology Handbook*"; contains fundamental theory of "*Beta-Defragmentation*" and "*Route-2*" systematic processing methodology.

cuneiform : the oldest extant writing system at the inception of modern civilization in Mesopotamia; a system of wedge-shaped script inscribed on clay tablets with a reed pen, allowing advancements in record keeping and communication no longer restricted to more literal graphic representations or pictures.

defragmentation : the *reparation* of wholeness; collecting all dispersed parts to reform an original whole; a process of removing "*fragmentation*" in data or knowledge to provide a clear understanding; applying techniques and processes that promote a *holistic* interconnected *alpha* state, favoring observational *Awareness* of continuity in all spiritual and physical systems; in *NexGen Systemology*, a "*Seeker*" achieving an actualized state of basic "*Self-Honest Awareness*" is said to be *beta-defragmented*, whereas *Alpha-defragmentation* is the rehabilitation of the *creative ability*, managing the *Spiritual Timeline* and the POV of *Self* as Alpha-Spirit (I-AM); see also "*Beta-defragmentation.*"

degree : a physical or conceptual *unit* (or point) defining the variation present relative to a *scale* above and below it; any stage or extent to which something *is* in relation to other possible positions within a *set* of "*parameters*"; a point within a specific range or spectrum; in *NexGen Systemology*, a *Seeker's* potential energy variations or fluctuations in thought, emotional reaction and physical perception are all treated as "*degrees.*"

demographics : segments of the population uniquely identified, whether real or representative; targeting a specific portion of the population, such as for marketing or statistics.

destiny : what is set down, made firm, standard, or stands fixed as a constant end; the absolute *destination* regardless of whatever course is traveled; in *NexGen Systemology*, the "*destiny*" of the "*Human Spirit*" (or "*Alpha Spirit*") is infinite existence—"*Immortality.*"

dichotomy : a division into two parts, types or kinds.

differentiation : an apparent difference between aspects or concepts.

discernment : to perceive, distinguish and/or differentiate experience into true knowledge.

displace : to compel to leave; to move or replace something with something else in its place or space.

dissonance : discordance; out of step; out of phase; disharmonious; the "differential" between the way things are and the way things are experienced; cognitive dissonance could be demonstrated as A = abc, or C = A, the duplication of truth/communication is not A-for-A.

dynamic (systems) : a principle or fixed system which demonstrates its *'variations'* in activity (or output) only in constant relation to variables or fluctuation of interrelated systems; a standard principle, function, process or system that exhibits *'variations'* and change simultaneously with all connected systems.

Eastern traditions : the evolution of the *Ancient Mystery School* east of its origins, primarily the Asian continent, or what is archaically referred to as "oriental."

echelon : a level or rung on a ladder; a rank or level of command.

emotional encoding : the substance of *imprints*; associations of sensory experience with an *imprint*; perceptions of our environment that receive an *emotional charge*, which form or reinforce facets of an *imprint*; perceptions recorded and stored as an *imprint* within the "emotional range" of energetic manifestation; the formation of an energetic store or charge on a channel that fixes emotional responses as a mechanistic automation, which is carried on in an individual's spiritual timeline or personal continuum of existence.

encompassing : to form a circle around, surround or envelop around.

enforcement : the act of compelling or putting (effort) into force; to compel or impose obedience by force; to impress strongly with applications of stress to demand agreement or validation; the lowest-level of direct control by physical effort or threat of punishment; a low-level method of control in the absence of true communication.

engineering : the *Self-directed* actions and efforts to utilize knowledge (observed causality/science), maths (calculations/quantification) and logic (axioms/formulas) to understand, design or manifest a solid structure, machine, mechanism, engine or system; as "*Reality Engineering*" in *NexGen Systemology*—intentional *Self-directed* adjustment of existing Reality conditions; the application of total *Self-determinism* in *Self-Honesty* to change apparent Reality using fundamentals of *Systemology* and *Cosmic Law.*

entropy : the reduction of organized physical systems back into chaos-continuity when their integrity is measured against space over time.

epicenter : the point from which shock-waves travel.

epistemology : a school of philosophy focused on the truth of knowledge *and* knowledge of truth; theories regarding validity and truth inherent in any structure of knowledge and reason.

erroneous : inaccurate; incorrect; containing error.

esoteric : hidden; secret; knowledge understood by a select few.

etching : to cut, bite or corrode with acid to produce a pattern.

evaluate : to determine, assign or fix a set value, amount or meaning.

existence : the *state* or fact of *apparent manifestation*; the resulting combination of the Principles of Manifestation: consciousness, motion and substance; continued *survival*; that which independently exists; the *'Prime Directive'* and sole purpose of all manifestation or Reality; the highest common intended motivation driving any "*Thing*" or *Life*.

existential : pertaining to existence, or some aspect or condition of existence.

exoteric : public knowledge or common understanding; the level of understanding and *Knowing* maintained by the "masses"; the opposite of *esoteric*.

experiential data : accumulated reference points we store as memory concerning our "experience" with Reality.

extant : in existence; existing.

exterior : outside of; on the outside; in *NexGen Systemology*, we mean specifically the POV of *Self* that is *'outside of'* the *Human Condition,* free of the physical and mental trappings of the Physical Universe; a metahuman range of considera-tion; see also *'Zu-Vision'*.

external : a force coming from outside; information received from outside sources; in *NexGen Systemology*, the objective *'Physical Universe'* existence, or *beta-existence*, that the Phys-ical Body or *genetic vehicle* is essentially *anchored* to for its considerations of locational space-time as a dimension or POV.

extropy : in *NexGen Systemology*—the reduction of organized spiritual systems back into a singularity of Infinity when their integrity is measured against space over time.

facets : an aspect, an apparent phase; one of many faces of something; a cut surface on a gem or crystal; in *NexGen Sys-temology*—a single perception or aspect of a memory or "*Imprint*"; any one of many ways in which a memory is recor-ded; perceptions associated with a painful emotional (sensation) experience and "*imprinted*" onto a metaphoric lens through which to view future similar experiences; other sec-ondary terminals that are associated with a particular terminal, painful event or experience of loss, and which may exhibit the same encoded significance as the activating event.

faculties : abilities of the mind (individual) inherent or de-veloped.

fallacy : a deceptive, misleading, erroneous and/or false be-liefs; unsound logic; persuasions, invalidation or enforcement of Reality agreements based on authority, sympathy, band-wagon/mob mentality, vanity, ambiguity, suppression of information, and/or presentation of false dichotomies.

fate : what is brought to light or actualized as experience; the actual *course* taken to reach an end, charted end, or final *dest-*

ination; in *NexGen Systemology*, the *'fate'* of a *'Human Spirit'* (or *'Alpha Spirit'*) is determined by the choice of course taken to experience *Life*.

feedback loop : a complete and continuous circuit flow of energy or information directed as an output from a source to a target which is altered and return back to the source as an input; in *General Systemology*—the continuous process where outputs of a system are routed back as inputs to complete a circuit or loop, which may be closed or connected to other systems/circuits; in *NexGen Systemology*—the continuous process where directed *Life* energy and *Awareness* is sent back to *Self* as experience, understanding and memory to complete an energetic circuit as a loop.

flattening a wave : see *"process-out"* for definition; also see *"collapsing a wave."*

flow : movement across (or through) a channel (or conduit); a direction of active energetic motion typically distinguished as either an *in-flow*, *out-flow* or *cross-flow*.

fractal : a wave-curve, geometric figure, form or pattern, with each part representative of the same characteristics as the whole; any baseline, sequence or pattern where the 'whole' is found in the 'parts' and the 'parts' contain the 'whole'; a pattern that reoccurs similarly at various scales/levels on a continuous whole; a subset of a Euclidean space explored in higher-level academic mathematics, in which fractal dimensions are found to exceed topological ones; in NexGen Systemology, a "fractal-like" description is used specifically for a pattern or form that has a reoccurring nature without regard to what level or scale it is manifest upon. Examples include the formation of crystals, tree-like patterns, the comparison of atoms to solar systems to galaxies, &tc.

fragmentation : breaking into parts and scattering the pieces; the *fractioning* of wholeness or the *fracture* of a holistic interconnected *alpha* state, favoring observational *Awareness* of perceived connectivity between parts; *discontinuity*; separation of a totality into parts; in *NexGen Systemology*, a person outside a state of *Self-Honesty* is said to be *fragmented*.

game : a strategic situation where a "player's" power of choice is employed or affected; a parameter or condition defined by purposes, freedoms and barriers (rules).

game theory : a mathematical theory of logic pertaining to strategies of maximizing gains and minimizing loses within prescribed boundaries and freedoms; a field of knowledge widely applied to human problem solving and decision-making; the application of true knowledge and logic to deduce the correct course of action given all variables and interplay of dynamic systems; logical study of decision making where "players" make choices that affect (the interests) of other "players"; an intellectual study of conflict and cooperation.

general systemology ("systematology") : a methodology of analysis and evaluation regarding the systems—their design and function; organizing systems of interrelated information-processing in order to perform a given function or pattern of functions.

genetic memory : the evolutionary, cellular and genetic (DNA) "memory" encoded into a *genetic vehicle* or *living organism* during its progression and duplication (reproduction) over millions (or billions) of years on Earth; in *NexGen Systemology*—the past-life Earth-memory carried in the genetic makeup of an organism (*genetic vehicle*) that is *independent of any* actual "spiritual memory" maintained by the *Alpha Spirit* themselves, from its own previous lifetimes on Earth and elsewhere using other *genetic vehicles* with no direct evolutionary connection to the current physical form in use.

genetic-vehicle : a physical *Life*-form; the physical (*beta*) body that is animated/controlled by the (*Alpha*) *Spirit* using a continuous *Lifeline* (ZU); a physical (*beta*) organic receptacle and catalyst for the (*Alpha*) *Self* to operate "causes" and experience "effects" within the *Physical Universe*.

gnosis : a *Greek* word meaning knowledge, but specifically "true knowledge"; the highest echelon of "true knowledge" accessible (or attained) only by mystical or spiritual faculties whereby actualized realizations are achieved independent of specialized education.

Gnostics : a name meaning "having knowledge" in Greek language (see also *gnosis*); an early sect of Judeo-Christian mysticism from the 1st Century AD emphasizing true knowledge by *Self-Honest* experience of metahuman and spiritual states of beingness, emphasizing defragmentation of "illusion" and overcoming of material "deception"; an esoteric proto-Systemology organization disbanded by the Roman Church as heretical.

gradient : a degree of partitioned ascent or descent along some scale, elevation or incline; "higher" and "lower" values in relation to one another.

holistic : the examination of interconnected systems as encompassing something greater than the *sum* of their "parts."

Homo Novus : literally, the "new man"; the "newly elevated man" or "known man" in ancient Rome; the man who "knows (only) through himself"; in NexGen Systemology—the next spiritual and intellectual evolution of *homo sapiens* (the "modern Human Condition"), which is signified by a demonstration of higher faculties of *Self-Actualization* and clear *Awareness*.

Homo Sapiens Sapiens : the present standard-issue Human Condition; the *hominid* species and genetic-line on Earth that received modification, programming and conditioning by the *Anunnaki* race of *Alpha-Spirits*, of which early alterations contributed to various upgrades (changes) to the genetic-line, beginning approximately 450,000 years ago (*ya*) when the *Anunnaki* first appear on Earth; a species for the Human Condition on Earth that resulted from many specific *Anunnaki* "genetic" and "cultural" *interventions* at certain points of significant advancement—specifically (but not limited to) *circa* 300,000 *ya*, 200,000 *ya*, 40,000 *ya,* and 8,000 *ya*; a species of the Human Condition set for replacement by *Homo Novus*.

Human Condition : a standard default state of Human experience that is generally accepted to be the extent of its potential identity (*beingness*)—currently treated as *Homo Sapiens Sapiens,* but which is scheduled for replacement by *Homo Novus*.

identification : the association of *identity* to a thing; a label or fixed data-set associated to what a thing is; association "equals" a thing, the "equals" being key; an equality of all things in a group, for example, an "apple" identified with all other "apples"; the reduction of "I-AM"-*Self* from a *Spiritual Beingness* to an "identity" of some form.

identity : the collection of energy and matter—including memory—across a *"Spiritual Timeline"* that we consider as "I" of *Self*, but the "I" is an individual and not an identification with anything other than *Self* as *Alpha-Spirit*.

identity-system : the application of the *ZU-line* as "I"—the continuous expression of *Self* as *Awareness* across a *"Spiritual Timeline"*; see *"identity."*

imagination : the ability to create *mental imagery* in one's Personal Universe at will and change or alter it as desired; the ability to create, change and dissolve mental images on command or as an act of will; to create a mental image or have associated imagery displayed (or "conjured") in the mind that may or may not be treated as real (or memory recall) and may or may not accurately duplicate objective reality; to employ *Creative Abilities* of the Spirit that are independent of reality agreements with beta-existence.

immersion : plunged or sunk into; wholly surrounded by.

implant : to graft or surgically insert; to establish firmly by setting into; to instill or install a direct command or consideration in consciousness (Mind-System, &tc.); a mechanical device inserted beneath the surface/skin; in *Metahuman Systemology*, an "energetic mechanism" (linked to an Alpha-Spirit) composing a circuit-network and systematic array of energetic receptors underlying and filter-screening communication channels between the Mind-System and *Self*; an energetic construct installed upon entry of a Universe; similar to a platen or matrix or circuit-board, where each part records a specific type or quality of *emotionally encoded imprints* and other "heavily charged" *Mental Images* that are "impressed" by future encounters; a basic platform on which certain *imprints* and *Mental Images* are encoded (keyed-in) and stored (often beneath the surface of "knowing" or *Awareness* for that individual, although an implanted "command" toward certain inclinations or behavioral tendencies may be visibly observable.

imprint : to strongly impress, stamp, mark (or outline) onto a softer 'impressible' substance; to mark with pressure onto a surface; in *NexGen Systemology*, the term is used to indicate permanent Reality impressions marked by frequencies, energies or interactions experienced during periods of emotional distress, pain, unconsciousness, loss, enforcement, or something antagonistic to physical (personal) survival, all of which are are stored with other reactive response-mechanisms at lower-levels of *Awareness* as opposed to the active memory database and proactive processing center of the Mind; an experiential "memory-set" that may later resurface—be triggered or stimulated artificially—as Reality, of which similar responses will be engaged automatically; holographic-like imagery "stamped" onto consciousness as composed of energetic *facets* tied to the "snap-shot" of an experience.

imprinting incident : the first or original event instance communicated and *emotionally encoded* onto an individual's *"Spiritual Timeline"* (recorded memory from all lifetimes), which formed a permanent impression that is later used to mechanistically treat future contact on that channel; the first or original occurrence of some particular *facet* or mental image related to a certain type of *encoded response*, such as pain and discomfort, losses and victimization, and even the acts that we have taken against others along the Spiritual Timeline of our existence that caused them to also be *Imprinted*.

incarnation : a present, living or concrete form of some thing or idea; an individual lifetime or life-cycle from birth/creation to death/destruction independent of other lifetimes or cycles.

inception : the beginning, start, origin or outset.

incite : to urge on or cause; instigate; prove or stimulate into action.

individual : a person, lifeform, human entity or creature; a *Seeker* or potential *Seeker* is often referred to as an "individual" within Mardukite Zuism and Systemology materials.

infinite existence : "immortality."

inhibited : withheld, discouraged or repressed from some state.

"in phase" : see *"phase alignment."*

institution : a social standard or organizational group responsible for promoting some system or aspect in society.

intention : the directed application of Will; to intend (have "in Mind") or signify (give "significance" to) for or toward a particular purpose; in *NexGen Systemology* (from the *Standard Model*)—the spiritual activity at WILL (5.0) directed by an *Alpha Spirit* (7.0); the application of WILL as "Cause" from a higher order of Alpha Thought and consideration (6.0), which then may continue to relay communications as an "effect" in the universe.

interior : inside of; on the inside; in *NexGen Systemology*, we mean specifically the POV of *Self* that is fixed to the *'internal' Human Condition,* including the *Reactive Control Center* (RCC) and Mind-System or *Master Control Center* (MCC); within *beta-existence*.

intermediate : a distinct point between two points; actions between two points.

internal : a force coming from inside; information received from inside sources; in *NexGen Systemology*, the objective *'Physical Universe'* experience of *beta-existence* that is associated with the Physical Body or *genetic vehicle* and its POV regarding sensation and perception; from inside the body; within the body.

invalidate : decrease the level or degree or *agreement* as Reality.

invests : spends on; gives or devotes something to earn a result; endows with.

"kNow" : a creative spelling and use of semantics for "know" and "now" to indicate the state of present-time actualized "Awareness" as Self (Alpha-Spirit), developed for dual-meaning messages made by early Mardukite Systemologists in 2008-9, such as "live in the kNow" or "be in the kNow" and even "drown in the kNow" &tc.

knowledge : clear personal processing of informed understanding; information (data) that is actualized as effectively workable understanding; a demonstrable understanding on which we may 'set' our *Awareness*—or literally a "knowledge."

KI : an ancient cuneiform sign designating the *'physical zone'*; the *Physical Universe*—comprised of physical matter and physical energy in action across space and observed as time; a direction of motion toward material *Continuity*, away from or subordinate to the Spiritual (*'AN'*); the physical condition of existence providing for our *beta* state of *Awareness* experienced (and interacted with) as an individual *Lifeform* from our primary Alpha state of Identity or *I-AM-Self* in the *Spiritual Universe* (*'AN'*).

level : a physical or conceptual *tier* (or plane) relative to a *scale* above and below it; a significant *gradient* observable as a *foundation* (or surface) built upon and subsequent to other levels of a totality or whole; a *set* of "*parameters*" with respect to other such *sets* along a *continuum*; in *NexGen Systemology*, a *Seeker's* understanding, *Awareness* as *Self* and the formal grades of material/instruction are all treated as "*levels*."

Liber-One : First published in October 2019 as "*The Tablets of Destiny: Using Ancient Wisdom to Unlock Human Potential*" by Joshua Free; republished in the complete *Grade-III* anthology, "*The Systemology Handbook.*"

Liber-2B : First published in December 2019 as "*Crystal Clear: The Self-Actualization Manual & Guide to Total Awareness*" by Joshua Free; republished in the complete *Grade-III* anthology, "*The Systemology Handbook.*"

logic equations : using symbols and basic mathematical logic to establish the validity of statements or to see how a variable within a system will change the result; a basic demonstration of proportion or relationship between variables in a system.

manifestation : something brought into existence.

Marduk : founder of Babylonia; patron Anunnaki "god" of Babylon.

Mardukite Zuism : a Mesopotamian-themed (Babyloni-an-oriented) religious philosophy and tradition applying the spiritual technology based on *Arcane Tablets* in combination with "Tech" from *NexGen Systemology*; first developed in the New Age underground by Joshua Free in 2008 and realized publicly in 2009 with the formal establishment of the *Mardukite Chamberlains.* The text *"Tablets of Destiny"* is a cross-over from Mardukite Zuism (and Mesopotamian Neopaganism) toward higher spiritual applications of Systemology.

Master-Control-Center (MCC) : a perfect computing device to the extent of the information received from "lower levels" of sensory experience/perception; the proactive communication system of the *"Mind"*; a relay point of active *Awareness* along the Identity's *ZU-line*, which is responsible for maintaining basic *Self-Honest Clarity* of *Knowingness* as a *seat of consciousness* between the *Alpha-Spirit* and the secondary *"Reactive Control Center"* of a *Lifeform* in *beta existence*; the Mind-center for an *Alpha-Spirit* to actualize cause in the *beta existence*; the analytical *Self-Determined* Mind-center of an *Alpha-Spirit used* to project *Will* toward the genetic body; the point of contact between *Spiritual Systems* and the *beta existence*; presumably the *"Third Eye"* of a being connected directly to the *I-AM-Self*, which is responsible for *determining* Reality at any time; in *NexGen Systemology*, this is plotted at (4.0) on the continuity model of the *ZU-line*.

mental image : a subjectively experienced "picture" created and imagined into being by the Alpha-Spirit (or at lower levels, one of its automated mechanisms) that includes all perceptible *facets* of totally immersive scene, which may be forms originated by an individual, or a "facsimile-copy" ("snap-shot") of something seen or encountered; a duplication of wave-forms in one's Personal Universe as a "picture" that mirror an "external" Universe experience, such as an *Imprint*.

Mesopotamia : land between Tigris and Euphrates River;

modern-day Iraq; the primary setting for ancient *Sumerian* and *Babylonian* traditions thousands of years ago, including activities and records of the *Anunnaki*.

metahumanism : an applied philosophy of *transhumanism* with an emphasis on "spiritual technologies" as opposed to "external" ones; a new state or evolution of the *Human Condition* achievable on planet Earth, rooted in *Self-Honesty*, whereby individuals are operating *exterior* to considerations that are fixed exclusively to the *genetic vehicle* (Human Body) and independent of the *emotional encoding* and *associative programming* typical of the present standard-issue *Human Condition*.

methodology : a system of methods, principles and rules to compose a systematic paradigm of philosophy or science.

misappropriated : put into use incorrectly; to apply ineffectively or as unintended by design.

motor functions : internal mechanisms that allow a body to move.

Nabu : the original "god of wisdom, writing and knowledge." (Babylonian)

neurotransmitter : a chemical substance released at a physiological level (of the genetic vehicle) that bridges communication of energetic transmission between the *Mind-Body* systems, using the "nervous system" of the physical body; biochemical amino acids and peptides (neuropeptides), hormones, &tc.

NexGen Systemology : a modern tradition of applied religious philosophy and spiritual technology based on *Arcane Tablets* in combination with "*general systemology*" and "*games theory*" developed in the New Age underground by Joshua Free in 2011 as an advanced futurist extension of the "*Mardukite Chamberlains*"; also referred to as "Mardukite Systemology," "Metahuman Systemology" and "Spiritual Systemology."

objectively : concerning the "external world" and attempts to observe Reality independent of personal "subjective" factors.

one-to-one : see "*A-for-A.*"

optimum : the most favorable or ideal conditions for the best result; the greatest degree of result under specific conditions.

organic : as related to a physically living organism or carbon-based life form; energy-matter condensed into form as a focus or POV of Spiritual Life Energy (*ZU*) as it pertains to beta-existence of *this* Physical Universe (*KI*).

pantheism : religious philosophies that observe God as inherent within all aspects of the Physical Universe.

paradigm : an all-encompassing *standard* by which to view the world and *communicate* Reality; a standard model of reality-systems used by the Mind to filter, organize and interpret experience of Reality.

parameters : a defined range of possible variables within a model, spectrum or continuum; the extent of communicable reach capable within a system or across a distance; the defined or imposed limitations placed on a system or the functions within a system; the extent to which a Life or "thing" can *be*, *do* or *know* along any channel within the confines of a specific system or spectrum of existence.

paramount : the most important; of utmost importance; "above all else."

participation : being part of the action; affecting the result.

patterns (probability patterns) : observation of cycles and tendencies to predict a causal relationship or determine the actual condition or flow of dynamic energy using a holistic systemology to understand Life, Reality and Existence as opposed to isolating or excluding perceived parts as being mutually separate from other perceived parts.

personality (program) : the total composite picture an individual "identifies" themselves with; the accumulated sum of material and mental mass by which an individual experiences as their timeline; a "beta-personality" is mainly attached to the identity of a particular physical body and the total sum of its own genetic memory in combination with the data stores and pictures maintained by the Alpha Spirit; a "true personality" is the Alpha Spirit as Self completely defragmented of all erroneous limitations and barriers to consideration, belief, manifestation and intention.

perturbation : the deviation from a natural state, fixed motion, or orbit system caused by another external system; disturbing or disquieting the serenity of an existent state; inciting observable apparent action using indirect or outside actions or 'forces'; the introduction of a new element or facet that disturbs equilibrium of a standard system; the "butterfly effect"; in *NexGen Systemology*, *'perturbation'* is a necessary condition for the *ZU-line* to function as a *Standard Model* of actual *'monistic continuity'*—which is a *Lifeforce* singularity expressed along a spectrum with potential interactions at each degree from any source; the influence of a degree in one state by activities of another state that seem independent, but which are actually connected directly at some higher degree, even if not apparently observed.

phase (identification) : in *NexGen Systemology,* a pattern of personality or identity that is assumed as the POV from *Self*; personal identification with artificial "personality packages"; an individual assuming or taking characteristics of another individual (often unknowingly as a response-mechanisms); also *"phase alignment."*

phase alignment or *"in phase"* : to be in synch or mutually synchronized, in step or aligned properly with something else in order to increase the total strength value; in *NexGen Systemology*, alignment or adjustment of *Awareness* with a particular identity, space or time; perfect *defragmentation* would mean being "in phase" as *Self* fully conscious and Aware as an Alpha-Spirit *in* present *space* and *time*, free of synthetic personalities.

physics : regarding data obtained by a material science of observable motions, forces and bodies, including their apparent interaction, in the Physical Universe (specific to this *beta-existence*).

physiology : a material science of observable biological functions and mechanics of living organisms, including codification and study of identifiable parts and apparent systematic processes (specific to agreed upon makeup of the *genetic vehicle* for this *beta-existence*).

pilot : a professional steersman responsible for healthy functional operation of a ship toward a specific destination; in *NexGen Systemology*, an intensive trained individual qualified to specially apply *Systemology Processing* to assist other *Seekers* on the *Pathway*.

ping : a short, high pitched ring, chime or noise that alerts to the presence of something; in computer systems, a query sent on a network or line to another terminal in order to determine if there is a connection to it; in *NexGen Systemology*, the sudden somatic twinge or pain or discomfort that is felt as a sensation in the body when a particular terminal (lifeform, object, concept) is 'brought to mind' or contacted on a personal communication channel-circuit; the accompanying sensations and mental images that are experienced as an automatic-response to the presence of some channel or terminal.

player (game theory) : an individual that is making decisions in a game and/or is affected by decisions others are making in the game, especially if those other-determined decisions now affect the possible choices.

point-of-view (POV) : a point to view from; an opinion or attitude as expressed from a specific identity-phase; a specific standpoint or vantage-point; a definitive manner of consideration specific to an individual phase or identity; a place or position affording a specific view or vantage; circumstances and programming of an individual that is conducive to a particular response, consideration or belief-set (paradigm); a position (consideration) or place (location) that provides a specific view or perspective (subjective) on experience (of the objective).

postulate : to put forward as truth; to suggest or assume an existence *to be*; to provide a basis of reasoning and belief; a basic theory accepted as fact; in *NexGen Systemology*, "Alpha-Thought"—the top-most decisions or considerations made by the Alpha-Spirit regarding the "*is-ness*" (what things "are") about energy-matter and space-time.

potentiality : the total "sum" (collective amount) of "latent" (dormant—present but not apparent) capable or possible realizations; used to describe a state or condition of what has not yet manifested, but which can be influenced and predicted based on observed patterns and, if referring to beta-existence, Cosmic Law.

POV : see *"point-of-view."*

prehistoric : any time before human history is written; prior to c. 4000 B.C.

premise : a basis or statement of fact from which conclusions are drawn.

presence : the quality of some thing (energy/matter) being "present" in space-time; personal orientation of *Self* located in space and time and handling the energy-matter present.

prevalent : of wide extent; an extensive or largely accepted aspect or current state.

"process-out" or **"flatten a wave"** : to reduce *emotional encoding* of an *imprint* to zero; to dissolve a *wave-form* or *thought-formed* "solid" such as a *"belief"*; to completely run a *process* to its end, thereby *flattening* any previously *"collapsed-waves"* or *fragmentation* that is obstructing the *clear channel* of *Self-Awareness*; also referred to as "processing-out"; to discharge all previously held emotionally encoded imprinting or erroneous programming and beliefs that otherwise fix the free flow (wave) to a particular pattern, solid or concrete *"is"* form.

processing, systematic : the inner-workings or "through-put" result of systems; in *NexGen Systemology*, a methodology of applied spiritual technology used toward personal Self-Actualization; methods of selective directed attention, communicated language and associative imagery that targets an increase in personal control of the human condition.

projecting awareness : sending out (motion) or radiating *"consciousness"* from *Self* ("I") to another POV.

proportional : having a direct relationship or mutual interaction with.

reactive control center (RCC) : the secondary (reactive) communication system of the *"Mind"*; a relay point of *Awareness* along the Identity's *ZU-line*, which is responsible for engaging basic motors, biochemical processes and any *programmed automated responses* of a living *beta* organism; the reactive Mind-Center of a living organism relaying communications of *Awareness* between causal experience of *Physical Systems* and the *"Master Control Center"*; it presumably stores all emotional encoded imprints as fragmentation of "chakra" frequencies of *ZU* (within the range of the *"psychological/emotive systems"* of a being), which it may *react* to as Reality at any time; in *NexGen Systemology*, this is plotted at (2.0) on the continuity model of the *ZU-line*.

reality : see *"agreement."*

realization : the clear perception of an understanding; a consideration or understanding on what is "actual"; to make "real" or give "reality" to so as to grant a property of "being-ness" or "being as it is"; the state or instance of coming to an *Awareness*; in *NexGen Systemology*, "gnosis" or true knowledge achieved during *systematic processing*; achievement of a new (or "higher") cognition, true knowledge or perception of Self; a consideration of reality or assignment of meaning.

reasoning / rationality (game theory) : the extent to which a player seeks to play (make decisions, &tc.) in order to maximize the gains (or else survival) achievable within any given game conditions; the ability and willingness of an individual to reach toward conditions that promote the highest level of survival and existence and make the best choices and moves to see the desired goal manifest.

receptacle : a device or mechanism designed to contain and store a specific type of aspect or thing; a container meant to receive something.

relative : an apparent point, state or condition treated as distinct from others.

religion : a concise spiritual *paradigm*, set of beliefs and practices, regarding "Divinity," "Infinite Beingness"—or else, "God."

relinquish : to give up control, command or possession of.

repetitively : to repeat "over and over" again; or else "repetition."

responsibility : the *ability* to *respond*; the extent of mobilizing *power* and *understanding* an individual maintains as *Awareness* to enact *change*; the proactive ability to *Self-direct* and make decisions independent of an outside authority.

resurface : to return to, or bring up to, the "surface" what has been submerged; in *NexGen Systemology*—relating specifically to processes where a *Seeker* recalls blocked energy stored covertly as emotional "*imprints*" (by the RCC) so that it may be effectively defragmented from the "*ZU-line*" (by the MCC).

Seeker : an individual on the *Pathway to Self-Honesty*; a practitioner of *Mardukite Systemology* or *NexGen Systemology Processing* that is working toward *Spiritual Ascension*.

Self-actualization : bringing the full potential of the Human spirit into Reality; expressing full capabilities and creativeness of the *Alpha-Spirit*.

Self-determinism : the freedom to act, clear of external control or influence; the personal control of Will to direct intention.

Self-honesty : the basic or original *alpha* state of *being* and *knowing*; clear and present total *Awareness* of-and-as *Self*, in its most basic and true proactive expression of itself as *Spirit* or *I-AM*—free of artificial attachments, perceptive filters and other emotionally-reactive or mentally-conditioned programming imposed on the human condition by the systematized physical world; the ability to experience existence without judgment.

semantics : the *meaning* carried in *language* as the *truth* of a "thing" represented, *A-for-A*; the *effect* of language on *thought* activity in the Mind and physical behavior; language as *sym-*

bols used to represent a concept, "thing" or "solid."

semantic-set : the implied meaning behind any groupings of words or symbols used to define a specific paradigm.

sentient : a living organism with consciousness or intelligence; a "thinking" or "reasoning" being that perceives information from the "senses."

sine-wave : the *frequency* and amplitude of a quantified (calculable) *vibration* represented on a graph (graphically) as smooth repetitive *oscillation* of a *waveform*; a *waveform* graphed for demonstration—otherwise represented in *NexGen Systemology* logic equations as 'Wf,' or in mathematics as the *'function of x'* (*fx*); graphically representing arcs (*parameters*) of a circular *continuity* on a *continuum*; in the *Standard Model of NexGen Systemology*, the actual 'wave vibration' graphically displayed on an otherwise static *ZU-line* (of Infinity) is a *'sine-wave'*.

singularity : in general use, "to be singular," but our working definition suggests the opposite of individuality (contrary to most dictionaries); in upper-level sciences, a "zero-point" where a particular property or attribute is mathematically treated as "infinite" (such as the "black-hole" phenomenon), or else where apparently dissimilar qualities of all existing aspects (or individuals) share a "singular" expression, nature or quality; additionally, in *NexGen Systemology*, a hypothetical zero-point when apparent values of all parts in a Universe are equal to all other parts before it collapses; in *Transhumanism*, a hypothetical "runaway reaction" in technology, when it becomes self-aware, self-propagating, self-upgradable and self-sustainable, and replaces human effort of advancement or even makes continued human existence impossible; also, technological efforts to maintain an artificial immortality of the Human Condition on a digital mainframe.

slate : a hard thin flat surface material used for writing on; a chalk-board, which is a large version of the original wood-framed writing slate, named for the rock-type it was made from.

somatic : specifically pertaining to the physical body, its sensations and response actions or behaviors as separate from a "Mind-System"; also *"pings."*

space : a viewpoint or *Point-of-View* (POV) extended from any point out toward a dimension or dimensions; the consideration of a point or spot as an *anchor* or *corner* in addition to others, which collectively define parameters of a dimensional plane; the field of energy/matter mass created as a result of communication and control in action and measured as time (wave-length), such as "distance" between points (or peaks on a wave).

spectrum : a broad range or array as a continuous series or sequence; defined parts along a singular continuum.

spiritual timeline : a continuous stream of *Mental Images* or record of experiences that defines the "past" of a spiritual being (or *Alpha-Spirit*) and which includes impressions form all life-incarnations and significant spiritual events the being has encountered; also *"backtrack."*

standard issue : equally dispensed to all without consideration.

standard model : a fundamental *structure* or symbolic construct used to evaluate a complete *set* in *continuity* relative to itself and variable to all other *dynamic systems* as graphed or calculated by *logic*; in *NexGen Systemology*—our existential and cosmological cabbalistic model; a *"monistic continuity model"* demonstrating *total system* interconnectivity "above" and "below" observation of any apparent *parameters*; the *ZU-line* represented as a singular vertical (y-axis) waveform in space across dimensional levels (universes) without charting any specific movement across a dimensional time-graph x-axis.

static : characterized by a fixed or stationary condition; having no apparent change, movement or fluctuation.

successively : what comes after; forward into the future.

succumb : to give way, or give in to, a relatively stronger superior force.

Sumerian : ancient civilization of *Sumer*, founded in Mesopotamia c. 5000 B.C.

surefooted : proceeding surely; not likely to stumble or fall.

symbol : a concentrated mass with associated meaning or significance.

systematization : to arrange into systems; to systematize or make systematic.

Systemology : see *"NexGen Systemology."*

systems theory : see *"general systematology"*

Tablets of Destiny : the first professional publication of Mardukite Systemology, released publicly in October 2019; the first professional text in Grade-III Mardukite Systemology, released as *"Liber-One"* and reissued in the Grade-III Master Edition *"Systemology Handbook"*; contains fundamental theory of the *"Standard Model"* and *"Route-1"* systematic processing methodology.

terminal (node) : a point, end or mass on a line; a point or connection for closing an electric circuit, such as a post on a battery terminating at each end of its own systematic function; any end point or 'termination' on a line; a point of connectivity with other points; in systems, any point which may be treated as a contact point of interaction; anything that may be distinguished as an 'is' and is therefore a 'termination point' of a system or along a flow-line which may interact with other related systems it shares a line with; a point of interaction with other points.

thought-form : apparent *manifestation* or existential *realization* of *Thought-waves* as "solids" even when only apparent in Reality-agreements of the Observer; the treatment of *Thought-waves* as permanent *imprints* obscuring *Self-Honest Clarity* of *Awareness* when reinforced by emotional experience as actualized "thought-formed solids" (*"beliefs"*) in the Mind; energetic patterns that "surround" the individual.

thought-wave or **wave-form** : a proactive *Self-directed action* or reactive-response *action* of *consciousness*; the *process* of *thinking* as demonstrated in *wave-form*; the *activity* of *Awareness* within the range of *thought vibrations/frequencies* on the existential *Life-continuum* or *ZU-line*.

threshold : a doorway, gate or entrance point; the degree to which something is to produce an effect within a certain state or condition; the point in which a condition changes from one to the next.

thwarted : to successfully oppose or prevent a purpose from actualizing.

tier : a series of rows or levels, one stacked immediately before or atop another.

time : observation of cycles in action; motion of a particle, energy or wave across space; intervals of action related to other intervals of action as observed in Awareness; a measurable wave-length or frequency in comparison to a static state; the consideration of variations in space.

timeline : plotting out history in a linear (line) model to indicate instances (experiences) or demonstrate changes in state (space) as measured over time; a singular conception of continuation of observed time as marked by event-intervals and changes in energy and matter across space.

transmit : to send forth data along some line of communication; to move a point across a distance.

treat / treatment : an act, manner or method of handling or dealing with someone, something or some type of situation; to apply a specific process, procedure or mode of action toward some person, thing or subject; use of a specific substance, regimen or procedure to make an existing condition less severe; also, a written presentation that handles a subject in a specific manner.

turbulence : a quality or state of distortion or disturbance that creates irregularity of a flow or pattern; the quality or state of aberration on a line (such as ragged edges) or the emotional "turbulent feelings" attached to a particular flow or terminal node; a violent, haphazard or disharmonious commotion (such as in the ebb of gusts and lulls of wind action).

unconscious : a state when *Awareness* as *Self* is removed totally from the equation of *Life* experience, though it continues to be recorded in lower-level response mechanisms (fixed to a simulacrum or genetic vehicle) for later retrieval; see also *'biological unconsciousness'.*

understanding : a clear 'A-for-A' duplication of a communication as 'knowledge', which may be comprehended and retained with its significance assigned in relation to other 'knowledge' treated as a 'significant understanding'; the "grade" or "level" that a knowledge base is collected and the manner in which the data is organized and evaluated.

validation : reinforcement of agreements or considerations as "real."

vantage : a point, place or position that offers an ideal viewpoint (POV).

verbatim : precisely reproduced or duplicated communication, "word"-for-"word" (*'A-for-A'*)

vibration : effects of motion or wave-frequency as applied to any system.

viewpoint : see *"point-of-view" (POV).*

wave-form : see *"sine-wave."*

Western Civilization : modern contemporary culture, ideals, values and technology, particularly of Europe and North America as distinguished by growing urbanization, industrialization, and inspired by a history of rebellion to strong religious and political indoctrination.

will *or* **WILL** (5.0) : in *NexGen Systemology* (from the *Standard Model*), the Alpha-ability at "5.0" of a Spiritual Being (*Alpha Spirit*) at "7.0" to apply *intention* as "Cause" from consideration or Alpha-Thought at "6.0" that is superior to "beta-thoughts" that only manifest as reactive "effects" below "4.0" and *interior* to the *Human Condition.*

willingness : the state of conscious Self-determined ability and interest (directed attention) to *Be, Do* or *Have*; a Self-determined consideration to reach, face up to (*confront*) or manage some "mass" or energy; the extent to which an individual considers themselves able to participate, act or communicate along some line, to put attention or intention on the line, or to produce (create) an effect.

ZU : the ancient Sumerian cuneiform sign for the archaic verb —*"to know," "knowingness"* or *"awareness"*; in *Mardukite Zuism and Systemology*, the active energy/matter of the "Spiritual Universe" (AN) experienced as a *Lifeforce* or *consciousness* that imbues living forms extant in the "Physical Universe" (KI); *"Spiritual Life Energy"*; energy demonstrated by the WILL of an actualized *Alpha-Spirit* in the "Spiritual Universe" (AN), which impinges its *Awareness* into the Physical Universe (KI), animating/controlling *Life* for its experience of *beta-existence* along an individual Alpha-Spirit's personal *Identity-continuum*, called a *ZU-line*.

Zu-line : a theoretical construct in *Mardukite Zuism and Systemology* demonstrating *Spiritual Life Energy* (*ZU*) as a personal individual "continuum" of Awareness interacting with all Spheres of Existence on the Standard Model of Systemology; a spectrum of potential variations and interactions of a monistic continuum or singular *Spiritual Life Energy (ZU)* demonstrated on the Standard Model; an energetic channel of potential POV and "locations" of Beingness, demonstrated in early Systemology materials as an individual Alpha-Spirit's personal *Identity-continuum*, potentially connecting *Awareness (ZU)* of *Self* with *"Infinity"* simultaneous with all points considered in existence; a symbolic demonstration of the *"Life-line"* on which *Awareness (ZU)* extends from the direction of the "Spiritual Universe" (AN) in its true original *alpha state* through an entire possible range of activity resulting in its *beta state* and control of a *genetic-entity* occupying the *Physical Universe (KI)*.

Zu-Vision : the true and basic (*Alpha*) Point-of-View (perspective, POV) maintained by *Self* as *Alpha-Spirit* outside boundaries or considerations of the *Human Condition* "Mind-Systems" and *exterior* to beta-existence reality agreements with the Physical Universe; a POV of Self *as* "a unit of Spiritual Awareness" that exists independent of a "body" and entrapment in a *Human Condition*; "spirit vision" in its truest sense.

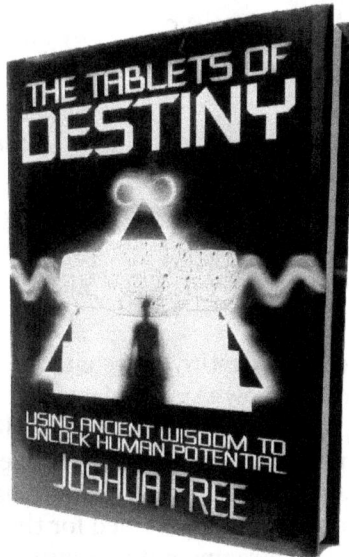

SYSTEMOLOGY
The Pathway to Self-Honesty

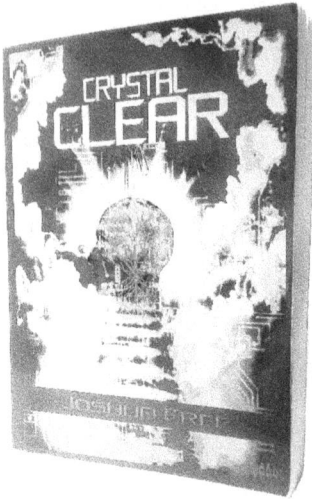

CRYSTAL CLEAR

The Self-Actualization Manual & Guide to Total Awareness

by Joshua Free
Foreword by Kyra Kaos

Mardukite Systemology Liber-2B

available in Paperback and Hardcover

Take control of your destiny and chart the first steps
toward your own spiritual evolution.
Realize new potentials of the Human Condition with
a Self-guiding handbook for Self-Processing
toward Self-Actualization in Self-Honesty using actual
techniques and training provided for the coveted
"Mardukite Self-Defragmentation Course Program"
—once only available directly and privately from the
underground International Systemology Society.

Discover the amazing power behind the
applied spiritual technology
used for counseling and advisement in
the Mardukite Zuism tradition.

SYS☥EMOLOGY
The Pathway to Self-Honesty

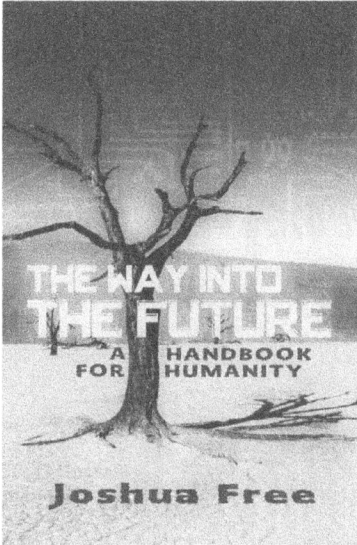

A Basic Introduction to Mardukite Systemology

THE WAY INTO THE FUTURE

Handbook for Humanity

a collection of writings by
Joshua Free
selected by James Thomas

available in Paperback and Hardcover

Here are the basic answers to what has held Humanity back from achieving its ultimate goals and unlocking the true power of the Spirit and highest state of Knowing and Being.

"The Way Into The Future" illuminates the *Pathway* leading to Planet Earth's true "metahuman" destiny. With *excerpts from "Tablets of Destiny," "Crystal Clear," "Systemology—Original Thesis"* and *"The Power of Zu."* You can help shine clear light on anyone's pathway!

Carefully selected by Mardukite Publications Officer, James Thomas, this critical *collection of eighteen articles, lecture transcripts and reference chapters* by Joshua Free is sure to be not only a treasured part of your personal library, but also the perfect introduction for all friends, family and loved ones.

(*Basic Grade-III Introductory Pocket Anthology*)

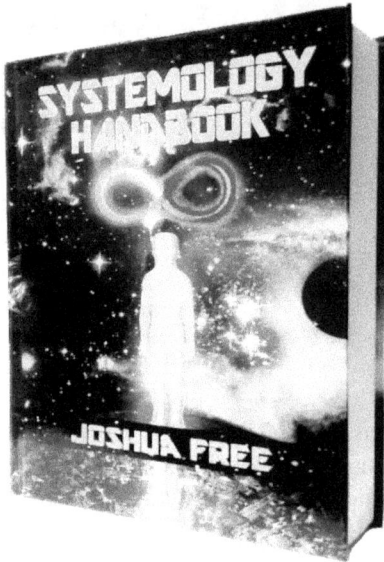

MARDUKITE
MASTER COURSE
Keys to the Gates of Higher Understanding

Now you can experience the Legendary "Master Course" from anywhere in the Universe, exactly as given in person by Joshua Free to the "Mardukite Academy of Systemology" in September 2020.

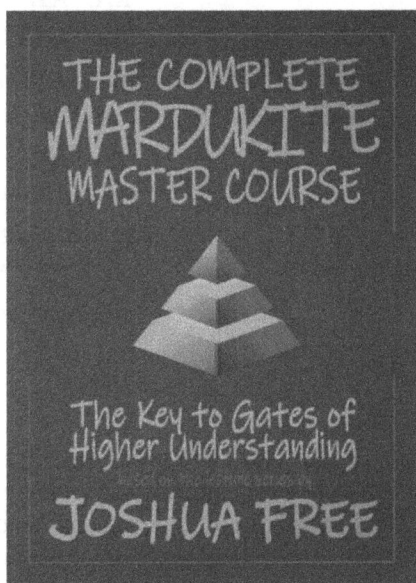

800+ pages of materials collected in this volume provide Seekers with full transcripts to all *48 Academy Lectures* of the legendary *"Mardukite Master Course"* combined with all course outlines, supplements and critical handouts from the original *"Instructor's Manual"*—making this the most complete definitive single-source delivery of New Age understanding and spiritual technology.

Referencing 25 years of research, development and publishing, including *"Necronomicon: The Complete Anunnaki Legacy,"* *"The Great Magickal Arcanum,"* *"The Systemology Handbook"* and *"Merlyn's Complete Book of Druidism."*

SYS†EMOLOGY
The Gateways to Infinity

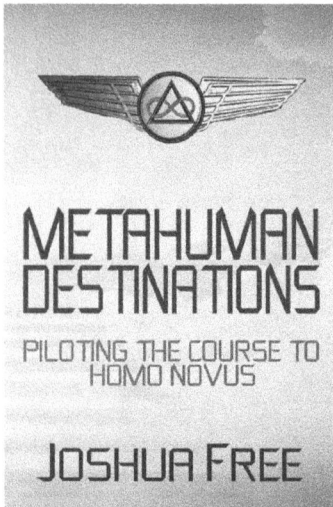

METAHUMAN DESTINATIONS

Piloting the Course to Homo Novus

by Joshua Free
Foreword by David Zibert

Mardukite Systemology Liber-Two

available in hardcover

Drawing from the Arcane Tablets and nearly a year of additional research, experimentation and workshops since the introduction of applied spiritual technology and systematic processing methods, Joshua Free provides the ground-breaking manual for those seeking to correct—or "defragment"—the conditions that have trapped viewpoints of the Spirit into programming and encoding of the Human Condition.

Experience the revolutionary professional course in advanced spiritual technology for Mardukite Systemologists to "Pilot" the way to higher ideals that can free us from the Human Condition and return ultimate command and control of creation to the Spirit.

SYSTEMOLOGY
The Gateways to Infinity

IMAGINOMICON

The Gateway to Higher Universes

A Grimoire for the Human Spirit

by Joshua Free

Mardukite Systemology Liber-3D

available in hardcover

The Way Out. Hidden for 6,000 Years.
But now we've found the Key.
A grimore to summon and invoke, command and control,
the most powerful spirit to ever exist.
Your Self.

Access beyond physical existence.
Fly free across all Gateways.
Go back to where it all began and reclaim that
personal universe which the *Spirit* once called *"Home."*

Break free from the Matrix;
command the Mind and control the Body
from outside those systems
— because *You* were never "human" —
fully realize what it means to be a *spiritual being*,
then rise up through the Gateways to Higher Universes
and *BE*.

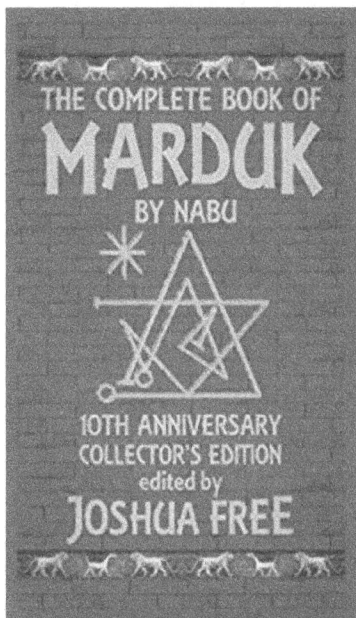

THE COMPLETE BOOK OF MARDUK BY NABU

A Pocket Anunnaki Devotional Companion to Babylonian Rituals

edited by Joshua Free

10th Anniversary
Collector's Edition Hardcover
Mardukite Liber-W

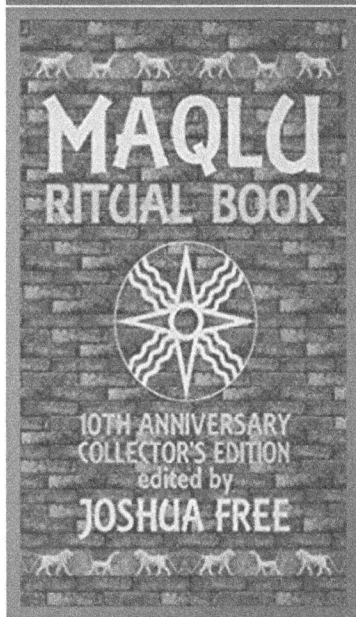

THE MAQLU RITUAL BOOK

A Pocket Companion to Babylonian Exorcisms, Banishing Rites & Protective Spells

edited by Joshua Free

10th Anniversary
Collector's Edition Hardcover
Mardukite Liber-M

The Original Classic Underground Bestseller Returns!
10th Anniversary Hardcover Collector's Edition.
Explore the original religion on Earth.

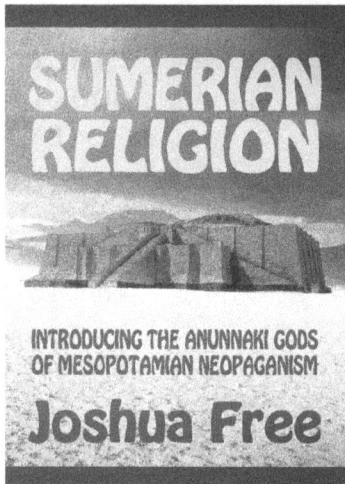

SUMERIAN RELIGION
Introducing the Anunnaki Gods
of Mesopotamian Neopaganism

Mardukite Research Volume Liber-50

by Joshua Free

Develop a personal relationship with Anunnaki Gods
—the divine pantheon that launched a thousand
cultures and traditions throughout the world!

Even if you think you already know all about the Sumerian Anunnaki or Star-Gates of Babylon... ∗ Here you will find a beautifully crafted journey that is unlike anything Humans have had the opportunity to experience for thousands of years... ∗ Here you will find a truly remarkable tome demonstrating a fresh new approach to modern Mesopotamian Neopaganism and spirituality... ∗ Here is a Master Key to the ancient mystic arts: true knowledge concerning the powers and entities that these arts are dedicated to... ∗ A working relationship with these powers directly... ∗ And the wisdom to exist "alongside" the gods, so as to ever remain in the "favor" of Cosmic Law.

Original underground classics.
Joshua Free's bestselling
"Druid Trilogy"

DRACONOMICON

The Book of Ancient Dragon Magick

25th Anniversary Hardcover
Collector's Edition

by Joshua Free

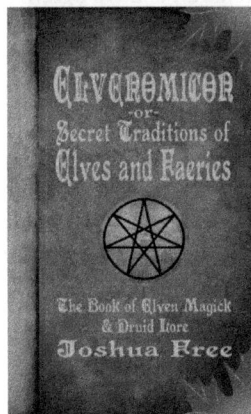

THE DRUID'S HANDBOOK

Ancient Magick for a New Age

20th Anniversary Hardcover
Collector's Edition

by Joshua Free

ELVENOMICON -or- SECRET TRADITIONS OF ELVES AND FAERIES

The Book of Elven Magick
& Druid Lore

15th Anniversary Hardcover
Collector's Edition

by Joshua Free

All three Grade-I Route-D titles
(...plus additional material...)
now available in the anthology:

Merlyn's Complete
Book of Druidism
by Joshua Free.

∞

19 95

JOSHUA FREE

20 20

PUBLISHED BY THE **JOSHUA FREE** IMPRINT REPRESENTING

The Founding Church of Mardukite Zuism
& Mardukite Academy of Systemology

SYS┃EMOLOGY

MARDUKITE
ZUISM

mardukite.com

www.ingramcontent.com/pod-product-compliance
Lightning Source LLC
Chambersburg PA
CBHW051845090426
42811CB00034B/2210/J